KB007967

Disney · PIXAR
ELEMENTAL

DISNEY·PIXAR
ELEMENTAL

Adapted by Erin Falligant

Prologue

A **board** a small boat, the **flaming outline**s of a Fire couple, a man and a woman, **illuminate**d the area around them. They excitedly **await**ed the view of the **shore**s of their new country. They traveled with only a few **possession**s from Fire Land, the home they'd left behind. A Blue **Flame contain**ed by a lantern[1] was the most **precious** item of all. The Flame **represent**ed their Fire Land **tradition**s and **heritage**.

The man **gently** placed a hand on his wife's round **belly**, **anticipating** the baby that would soon arrive. He **lean**ed in

---

1 lantern 랜턴. 손잡이가 달려 있어 들고 다닐 수 있는 등(燈).

to talk to it.

As the boat **head**ed toward shore, the man looked **into the distance**. **Element** City lay ahead—**skyscraper**s **top**ped with windmills,[2] buildings covered with trees, and high-speed **waterway**s. From every direction, **balloon**s, **blimp**s, and boats made their way toward the city's shore.

For the **citizen**s of Element City, it was a **typical** day. There were all kinds of people here—they were called Elements. Water Elements in **varying shade**s of blue **slosh**ed along **sidewalk**s. **Earth** Elements covered in grass, leaves, and **branch**es also filled the sidewalks. Air Elements shaped like colorful clouds **drift**ed past or blew by overhead.

As the boat **near**ed land, the man gently turned his wife to face the **shoreline**, showing the **baby-to-be** where they were headed.

He smiled just as the boat reached land. The couple stepped off the boat, **relieved** to be back on dry, **solid** ground.

Another boat **dock**ed **nearby**, filled with so many **leafy** Earth Elements that the ship's deck[3] looked like a forest had

---

2 **windmill** 풍차. 바람의 힘을 기계적인 힘으로 바꿔 동력을 얻는 장치.
3 **deck** 갑판. 규모가 큰 배 위에 나무나 철판으로 깔아 놓은 넓고 평평한 바닥.

sprouted on it. The **passengers filed** out through its gates.

A **submarine emerge**d, too, and water flowed out into a **puddle**. Suddenly, Water Elements began to take shape from the puddle, **gather**ing their **luggage**.

"I believe this is yours," said one Water passenger, holding out a **briefcase**.

"Thanks!" said another, taking the case. "Have a wetter day!**4**"

Overhead, a blimp **land**ed on a **perch**. A **gust** of air **shot** out of a **portal**, and Air Elements formed from the cloud. As they **disembark**ed, the blimp **deflate**d. Then more passengers **board**ed, and it **puff**ed back **up**.

The Fire couple followed the crowd of Earth, Water, and Air Elements into the **immigration hall**. They **pause**d to **admire** a **mural** that **depict**ed three Elements—Earth, Air, and Water—coming together to form Element City.

Fire was not among them.

The Fire couple waited in the long line of **immigrants making their way** through the hall. The other Elements

---

4 **have a wetter day** '좋은 하루 보내세요'라는 뜻의 인사말 'Have a nice day'를 물의 원소 입장에 맞게 바꾼 표현.

stepped away from the Fire couple's flaming forms. Water Elements feared being boiled, while Earth Elements worried their leaves and branches would go up in flames if they got too close.

At last, the Fire couple reached the front of the line.

"Next," called the immigration **official**.

The Fire couple hurried forward.

"Name?" asked the official.

The man responded in Firish,[5] the language of Fire Land, his words **sizzling** with excitement. *"Útrí dàr ì Bùrdì,"* he said.

"Fâsh ì Síddèr," the woman said.

The official didn't understand Firish. He thought for a moment and got an idea. "You know what? Let's just **go with** Bernie and . . . Cinder," said the immigration official, pressing his branch nose onto an ink pad and **stamp**ing a **document**. "Welcome to Element City!"

The Fire couple, now known as Bernie and Cinder Lumen, hurried out the doors into the **bustling** city. As they walked,

---

5 **Firish** '불의 종족의 언어'라는 뜻으로 'fire(불)'와 언어를 나타내는 접미사 '-ish'를 합쳐서 만들어 낸 단어.

they **gaze**d at the **canal**s, **waterfall**s, and giant plants that formed the city's **infrastructure**. It looked so different from Fire Land. They were a *long* way from home.

"Hot **log**s!**⁶**" called a **vendor**. "Hot logs for sale!"

Bernie turned to see Water Elements **gliding** about on **waterslide**s. Other Elements rode paddleboats[7] along the canals that ran between the city **block**s lined with skyscrapers. Bernie walked right over a **tiny** Earth Element. Bernie lifted his leg, but her leaf hair caught on fire. A tiny Earth man walking behind her tried to **extinguish** it without success. A Water person passing by **douse**d them with water from his hand. The Earth woman's hair fire went out and the Earth man sprouted new growth.

They continued walking down the busy street. **Distracted** by the **sight**s, Bernie walked right through an Air Element.

"Hey! Watch it, Sparky!**⁸**" cried the Air Element. His legs were **separate**d from his body. They kicked over Bernie and

---

6 **hot log** 불의 종족이 먹는 음식의 한 종류로, 길죽한 빵에 소시지를 끼워 만든 음식인 'hot dog(핫도그)'에 발음이 비슷한 'log(통나무)'를 넣어 재치있게 만들어 낸 말.

7 **paddleboat** 외륜선. 배의 몸체 외부에 달린 수레바퀴 모양의 추진기가 회전하며 물을 밀어내는 힘으로 움직이는 배.

8 **Sparky** 'spark(불꽃)'에서 파생된 말로, 여기에서는 불의 종족을 무례하게 부르는 호칭으로 쓰였다.

Cinder's **suitcase** and walked off, **rejoin**ing the upper body.

Before Bernie could **apologize**, a Wetro[9] train **zoom**ed overhead on an **elevated** track. As the train crossed a bridge, Bernie got an idea.

A few minutes later, he stood beside Cinder inside a **crowded** train car. The other passengers **shrank back** and **stare**d.

The narrow train car was not designed for Fire Elements.

When the train **lurch**ed, a Water guy **stumble**d, **splash**ing water onto Cinder. Bernie **gasp**ed. Water would **damage** her flames! As her doused flames sizzled, Bernie quickly fed her some wood from their luggage. Then he **glare**d at the Water guy.

"What?" the guy said with a **shrug**.

"Hmm," Bernie **grumble**d. "Water." This was going to be a long ride.

Bernie and Cinder exited the Wetro station in an Earth **neighborhood**. When they saw a For **Rent** sign in the window of an **upscale** brownstone[10] building, they hurried toward the

---

9 Wetro 'wet(축축한)'과 'metro(지하철)'를 합쳐서 만들어 낸 말로, 엘리멘트 시티의 지하철을 가리키는 고유 명사로 쓰였다.

10 brownstone 19세기 미국 동부 지역의 건축에서 많이 사용되던 적갈색의 퇴적암.

door. The owner, an old-growth Earth Element, opened the door and his eyes **widen**ed.

Cinder gave him a **hopeful** smile and waved hello. But when her flames **set** the owner's dry, leafy hair **on fire**, he quickly closed the door.

At another building, Cinder pushed a **buzzer**, which **instantly** caught fire. She blew it out before the owner, a Water Element, opened the door. But when the owner saw the Fire couple—and the **smolder**ing doorbell—they **slam**med the door shut.

One after another, homeowners turned them away. With each slam of the door, Bernie and Cinder grew more **discouraged**. But they kept walking.

When they reached a **run-down** neighborhood, they sat down to rest. **Dejected** and tired, they were about to **give up**. That was when Bernie **spot**ted a **shabby** building with a For Sale sign in front. Hope **flicker**ed in his **chest**.

Inside the old **structure**, Bernie's mind **race**d, full of ideas for their new home. He would turn the first floor into a shop, a **shrine** to Fire Land where they would sell **snack**s and **souvenir**s **inspired** by their **homeland**.

Plink! Water **drip**ped from a pipe above, **barely** missing Cinder's flames.

Bernie didn't notice. He **pace**d so excitedly that his feet burned through the floor, and he fell into the **basement**. "I'm okay!" he **holler**ed up through the **splinter**s. When Cinder saw his thumbs-up,[11] she smiled with **relief**.

They placed their Blue Flame lantern in the **hearth**.

Bernie and Cinder were home.

One evening, it began to rain outside. But inside, their new home felt **cozy**, warm, and full of love.

That night, Cinder **gave birth** to their baby.

The tiny Fire baby **lit up** the room.

"*Íkì ss ûr,*" Cinder **murmur**ed. "It's a girl."

"*Bê ss ksòrìf,*" said Bernie. "She's so perfect." He reached into the Blue Flame lantern and **scoop**ed up some flames to gently **pour** over the baby's head. She **coo**ed . . . and then **sneeze**d.

---

11 **thumbs-up** 엄지손가락을 치켜 올리는 행동으로, 주로 상대방을 칭찬하거나 상대방의 의견에 찬성하는 표시로 쓰인다.

Bernie laughed. He held Ember up so she could see the world around her. "Welcome, my Ember, to your new life," he said.

In the years that followed, Bernie and Cinder **adjust**ed to living in Element City. While they learned a new language and new ways of doing things, Bernie also taught Ember the language, values, and **custom**s of their homeland.

When Bernie carefully poured the Blue Flame into a **cauldron**, Ember's eyes **blaze**d with interest. "Our Blue Flame holds all our traditions and gives us the **strength** to burn bright," he explained.

Ember watched as the Flame shot up inside the cauldron.

"Do I burn as bright?" Bernie asked, **flex**ing **his muscle**s and **striking one silly pose** after another.

Ember **giggle**d. While her father pushed the cauldron against the wall, she rode on it and **cheer**ed him on.

Slowly but surely as Ember grew, the shop began to **take**

shape. Bernie added **shelving** and **repair**ed the walls. He was **eager** for the time when his store would be ready.

Soon Ember started helping Bernie with his daily tasks. One day, they made a sign for the front door. Bernie wrote FIREPLACE in large letters on the sign. Then Ember burned a flame design into it with her finger. When it was finished, Bernie climbed a **ladder** and hung the sign above the shop's **entrance**.

He climbed down the ladder and stood beside Ember, admiring their work. "This shop is the *dream* of our family," he said. "And someday it will all be yours."

Ember's eyes widened. From that moment on, *this* was what she would **strive** for, to be a good daughter and to **take over** the shop—her father's dream.

Chapter 1

A year later, it was opening day at Bernie's shop. The **lava java**[1] pot was full, and hot **log**s rolled on a **warmer**. Bernie stood behind the **counter** with Ember beside him.

Cinder **stock**ed **shelves nearby**. When a Fire **Element** entered, Bernie **greet**ed them. "Welcome! Everything here is **authentic**."

"Then I gotta try the kol nuts,[2]" said the customer.

"Kol nuts coming up!" said Bernie.

---

1 **java** 원래 인도네시아 자바 섬에서 재배된 원두로 만든 커피를 말하지만, 미국에서는 'espresso(에스프레소)'와 함께 일반적으로 '커피'를 가리키는 말로 쓰인다.
2 **kol nuts** 숯콩. 숯으로 만든 통나무를 한입 크기로 납작하게 눌러 만든 것으로 불의 종족이 먹는 간식의 한 종류.

While her father **rang up** the order, Ember **tap**ped the keys on her toy **cash register.**

"Good daughter," Bernie said warmly.

He and Ember **squeeze**d logs in their **palms** to make **bite-sized** pieces of kol nuts and placed them on a **plate**. Ember handed the plate to the customer.

"Someday this shop will all be mine!" she **announced** with **pride**.

Bernie **tousle**d his daughter's **flames**. "When you are ready," he said.

As time passed, more people **emigrate**d from Fire Land to the Firetown **district** of Element City. Bernie's shop grew busier. Most of the customers were Fire Elements, but sometimes other Elements shopped there, too. The busier the shop became, the more Ember helped out. She even **assist**ed Bernie with his **deliveries**. Ember **rode on his shoulders** as they **buzz**ed **around** town on a scooter.[3]

---

3 **scooter** 스쿠터. 앞쪽에 발판이 있고 지름 22cm 이하의 작은 바퀴가 두 개 달린 소형 오토바이.

"Delivery!" Bernie announced.

"Delivery!" Ember **echo**ed.

Soon she was old enough to make **lollipop**s, one of her favorite tasks.

On one busy afternoon, two Fire kids **approach**ed the counter. One of them ordered two lollipops, placing a few coins on the counter.

"I got it, *Àshfá!*" Ember told her father. She **melt**ed a lollipop with the heat from her hands. Then she blew into it, **sculpt**ing the pop into a glasslike bubble. While she worked, her **inner** fire **glow**ed happily. A rainbow-colored **halo** **shimmer**ed around her.

Ember formed flames at the top of the pop and used her finger to draw on a face. When she was done, the pop looked just like her customer! She **tweak**ed the nose and handed it to the Fire kid, who laughed with **delight**.

The Fire kid's friend **lean**ed over and tried to **lick** the pop.

"Hey!" **snap**ped the first kid.

Bernie smiled, until two Water teenagers entered the shop. The teens **track**ed water inside and **carelessly bump**ed into shelves.

Bernie **nod**ded at Ember. "Water," he **mutter**ed. "**Keep an eye on** them."

Ember zipped up her fire as if putting on **protective armor**. Then she **salute**d her father. She approached the teens, who were **pour**ing water onto some **flaming souvenir**s.

"Oops!" said one teen, **giggling** as if it were an accident.

"Oops!" said the other as the Blue Flame souvenir in his hand **sputter**ed and smoked.

Ember **blaze**d up beside them. "You **splash** it, you buy it!" she **growl**ed.

One of the Water teens began to boil from her heat. "Ahhh!" he cried. The souvenir **pop**ped out of his hand, and Ember caught it just **in time**.

The teens **slosh**ed out of the shop. Ember watched them go with a **satisfied** smile.

"You showed them, huh?" said Bernie. He **holler**ed out the door after the teens. "Nobody **water**s **down** fire!"

"Yeah!" called Ember.

A few years later, Cinder **restock**ed shelves while a Fire soap opera[4] played on the TV above the counter. "The truth is . . . ," a soap opera actress said **dramatically** on the screen. The customers in the shop **hung on her every word**.

Cinder finished folding a KISS ME, I'M FIRISH T-shirt. She **glance**d at the TV. "She's not in love with him," she guessed.

". . . I'm not in love with you!" said the soap opera actress.

The customers in the shop **gasp**ed.

"Ha! Knew it!" Cinder **boast**ed.

Behind the counter, Ember helped her father make kol nuts. Now that she was a teenager, she was even faster than him! While he **struggle**d to **compress** the logs into kol nuts, she **effortlessly stack**ed up a **pile** of the tasty burned nuts.

When a man with thick glasses approached, Ember **nudge**d her father. *"Àshfá,"* she said. "Customer."

Bernie **hesitate**d. "How about," he said, "you take it today."

"For real?" she asked, **beam**ing. She had been waiting to hear those words for a long time. She **wipe**d her hands on her **apron** and **took a** deep **breath** as she welcomed the customer.

"How can I help you?" she asked with a smile.

---

4   **soap opera** 연속극. 텔레비전이나 라디오에서 일정한 시간대에 조금씩 이어서 방송하는 극.

The customer placed a metal basket filled with items on the counter, next to a **bucket** of **sparkler**s. "All this," he said. "And sparklers are 'buy one, get one free'?"

"That's right!" said Ember.

"Great! I'll take the free one," said the customer. He **grab**bed a sparkler out of the bucket and lit it with his finger.

Ember laughed **nervously**. "Oh, no, see . . . you need to *buy* one to get one free." She **gently** took the sparkler from the customer's **grip**. Then she blew it out.

"But I just want the free one," he **insist**ed, taking another sparkler.

"Sorry," said Ember, **plaster**ing **on a smile**. "That's not how this works." She grabbed the sparkler from his hand and blew it out.

"But the customer is always right," he snapped.

"Not in this case . . . ," said Ember.

He took another sparkler. Ember took it away. He grabbed another, and she took it away. "Nope," she said, blowing out the sparklers. Soon she had a **bouquet** of **burned-out** sparklers in her hand. "Nope, nope, nope, nope, nope!"

"Just give me one for free!" **demand**ed the customer.

"That's not how this works!" Ember **bellow**ed. Her flames **flicker**ed, turning purple, and then . . .

KABOOM!

She **explode**d.

By the time the **blast clear**ed, the shopping basket on the counter had melted into a **smoky blob**. A black **scorch mark** was **streak**ed across the floor, and little fires burned throughout the shop.

"Oh!" said Bernie, hurrying over. He grabbed some sparklers from the bucket and **stuck** them into the **melty** blob. Then he blew on them to light them and handed the blob to the customer. "Happy birthday!"

Bernie walked a shocked Ember away from the counter. "What just happened?" he asked. "Why did you **lose your temper**?"

"I . . . I don't know," Ember sputtered. "He was pushing and pushing, and it just . . ."

"Calm, calm," said Bernie. "Sometimes customers can be **tough**. Just take a breath and make a **connection**."

Ember nodded.

"When you can do that and not lose your temper, then you

will be ready to **take over** the shop," said Bernie.

Ember forced a smile. She could do this. She *would* do this.

Chapter 2

Many years later, Ember still **recall**ed her father's words when she had a difficult customer—like right now.

Take a breath, *make a connection*, she told herself. But her face flamed bright red with **lick**s of purple. Take a breath, *make a connection* . . . She tried again. *Take a breath! MAKE A CONNECTION!*

Too late.

KABLAM! She **explode**d, **smash**ing the shop's glass **countertop**.

Ember waved the smoke away and **cast** an **apologetic** look at the shocked customer.

"Sorry," Ember said with an **embarrassed** laugh. "Sorry about that. Sorry, sorry."

Two Fire shop **regular**s, Flarry and Flarrietta sat nearby. "She almost went full purple!" said Flarrietta. "I've never seen anyone go full purple!"

"Sorry, everyone," called Ember as her father hurried over.

"Oh! Please forgive my daughter," Bernie added. "She burns bright, but sometimes *too* bright."

He blew out a burning flower on the customer's hat. "Nice hat, by the way," he said. "Let me make you a new **batch**! **On the house!**"

The customer **nod**ded. But she **turn**ed **on her heel** and walked away.

Bernie started making the kol nuts while Ember **scoop**ed up the broken glass.

"Sorry, *Àshfá*," she said. "I don't know why that one got away from me." She put the glass in her mouth and started **chew**ing.

"Oh, you are **tense** because of the big Red Dot Sale tomorrow," said her father. "It has us all at a **broil**."

"I guess," she **admit**ted. Ember finished chewing and

blew the glass into a long **glow**ing tube. She **flatten**ed the glass into a **pane**. "It's just . . . some of these customers get me all . . . *grrr*.[1]"

"I know, I know. Just do what we practiced," said her father. "You are *so* good at everything else."

"You're right," said Ember. "I'll get it. I just want you to rest." With one last **inhale**, she put the final **touch**es on the glass pane.

"Mm-hmm," she said, feeling proud of her work.

She **slid** the glass back into the countertop with a **satisfied sigh**. "Done."

Bernie continued to make kol nuts, but then he started **cough**ing.

"You okay?" asked Ember.

Bernie **sniff**ed. "Just tired."

"Let me help," **insist**ed Ember.

Bernie **caught his breath** while Ember finished making the nuts.

From across the shop Flarry called, "Bernie, that cough

---

1 grrr 답답함이나 분노, 짜증을 나타낼 때 으르렁거리며 내뱉는 소리.

is **terrible**."

"Almost as terrible as your cooking," said Flarrietta.

Bernie laughed. "*Ê . . . shútsh,*" he said. "Sheesh.[2]"

"When you gonna **put Ember out of her misery** and **retire**, huh?" asked Flarrietta. "Finally put her name on the sign out there?"

Ember listened. When *would* her father retire?

"She will take over when she's ready," Bernie simply replied.

Ember **crack**ed **a joke** to hide her **disappointment**. "And speaking of 'ready,' we are *more* than ready for you to actually *buy* something," she told Flarrietta, "if you'd ever get up off your lazy ash.[3]"

Everyone in the shop **burst** into laughter. "Oh!" they called. "Burn!"

Bernie smiled. "But she is *so* close," he admitted.

"I mean, she'll probably never do **deliveries** as quick as me . . ."

---

2 **sheesh** '쳇', '참나'라는 뜻으로 실망이나 분노, 불쾌감을 나타내는 표현.
3 **lazy ash** '게으른 사람'이라는 뜻의 속어 'lazy ass'에 발음이 비슷하고 불의 원소와 관련된 말인 'ash(재)'를 넣어, 물건은 사지 않고 계속 앉아서 재만 떨어 뜨리고 있는 손님을 나타내는 표현으로 사용했다.

Everyone laughed again.

". . . but actions speak louder than worms," he continued.

"Words," corrected Ember.

"Words!" Bernie **echo**ed.

"You don't think I can **beat** your record?" She picked up a timer, **crank**ing the dial. "Because I've been taking it easy on you so I don't hurt your feelings, Mr. **Smokestack**.[4] But game on!"

As the timer **tick**ed, Ember hurried to **pack** up the deliveries. Bernie watched, a proud smile flickering across his face.

---

4 **Mr. Smokestack** 주인공 버니가 기침을 할 때 매캐한 검은 연기를 내뿜는 모습을 굴뚝에 비유해 장난스럽게 부르는 표현.

Chapter 3

Cinder sat in her **cozy** office. As Firetown's **self-appointed matchmaker**, she had a **natural gift** for smelling love. She could tell, **without a doubt**, when two people might make a good **match** . . . or not.

Cinder **gaze**d across the table at a young, nervous Fire couple. "Before I see if you are a match," she began, "I will splash this on your heart to bring love to the **surface**."

She **stir**red a bowl of oil and splashed a few drops onto the couple. Their flames blazed red. Then the couple lit the two sticks that Cinder had set on the table.

"And I will read the smoke," continued Cinder. She **sniff**ed the **wisp**s of smoke rising from the sticks.

Just then, Ember threw open the curtains in the room.

Whoosh! The smoke **dissipate**d.

"Ember!" **scold**ed Cinder. "I'm doing a reading!"

"Sorry," said Ember. "Gotta **grab** some stuff. Going **for** Dad's record." She **race**d toward the boxes in a corner of the room.

"So . . . are we a match?" asked the Fire guy.

"It's true love!" Cinder **announce**d. "Which is more than I ever smelled on this one." She **shot** Ember a look.

Ember rolled her eyes. "Oh, goodie.[1] This ol' chestnut.[2]"

As Ember turned to leave, Cinder grabbed her daughter's arm and sniffed it. "Yup, nothing," Cinder **confirm**ed. "Just a loveless, sad future of sadness."

Ember pulled her arm free and started walking out of the room.

"Ember!" her mother called. "Work with me!"

Ember rolled her eyes again and **sigh**ed.

"You finding a match was my mother's **dying wish**!"

---

1 **goodie** '이런', '맙소사'라는 뜻으로 놀라움이나 곤혹스러움 등을 나타내는 표현.

2 **ol' chestnut** '케케묵은 이야기', '진부한 농담'이라는 뜻으로, 극작가 윌리엄 다이먼드(William Dimond)의 작품 '부러진 칼(The Broken Sword)'의 두 주인공이 밤(chestnut)과 관련된 이야기를 여러 번 반복하여 말한 것에서 유래했다. 'ol'(old)'는 그 뜻을 강조하기 위해 사용된 단어이다.

Cinder said, her voice **crackling**. She **remind**ed Ember of the day Ember's grandmother had died. "Promise me one thing. Marry Fire," her grandmother had said. And then . . . *poof!* She was gone.

"Nice try, Mom," said Ember. "Gotta go!"

When Cinder turned back toward the Fire couple, they were **embracing**. She **squirt**ed them with a **spray** bottle. "Save it for the wedding!" she **spat**.

"Hey!" the Fire guy **sputter**ed.

Outside the shop, Ember carried the boxes to her scooter. That was when Clod, a young **Earth** boy, **pop**ped out of a **planter**. His camo-colored[3] shirt matched the green grass **sprout**ing from his head.

"Yo, yo, yo, Ember!" he called.

"Yo, Clod. Can't talk. In a hurry," she said. "And don't let my dad catch you out here again."

"What?" he said, giving his hair a quick **comb** with a gardening fork. "He doesn't like my *land*scaping?[4]"

---

3 **camo-colored** '위장색의'라는 의미의 형용사. 'camo'는 'camouflage(위장)'의 줄임말로, 본래의 모습이 드러나지 않도록 가리거나 꾸미기 위한 색깔을 말한다.

4 **landscaping** 본래 식물 등을 이용하여 인공적으로 자연의 경치를 아름답게 다듬고 가꾸는 '조경'을 뜻하지만, 여기에서는 흙의 원소 입장에서 풀을 다듬고 손질하여 치장하는 것을 나타내는 말로 쓰였다.

"Uff," **groan**ed Ember at the joke. She **strap**ped the boxes to her scooter.

"Anyway," said Clod, "June **Bloom** is coming, and you just got to be my **date**. 'Cause check it out—I'm all **grown up!**" He lifted his arm, **reveal**ing a tiny flower that had sprouted in his **armpit**. He sniffed it. "And I smell *gooood*."

As Clod **pluck**ed the flower, he **let out** an "Ow!" Then he **knelt** on the **sidewalk** and offered it to Ember in a **grand gesture**.

"My queen."

Ember took the flower. *Poof!* It **burn**ed **to a crisp** in her hand. "Sorry, **buddy**," she said. "Elements don't mix."

Then she remembered—the timer was **tick**ing! "Flame! Gotta go!"

"Come on!" Clod **begg**ed. "Go to the festival with me! You *never* leave this part of town."

"That's because everything I need is right here," replied Ember.

Just then, a Wetro train passed overhead, sending water splashing down. Ember **glance**d up, **annoyed**, as she popped open her umbrella.

"Plus," she said, "this city wasn't made with Fire people in mind."

As the train crossed the bridge toward Element City, Ember closed the umbrella and climbed onto her scooter.

"Sorry," she told Clod, "but it'd take an act of God to get me to cross that bridge."

"An act of God,[5] or an act of . . . *Clod*?" He **waggle**d his **eyebrow**s.

Ember didn't **bother** to laugh. "Gotta run!" she said as she drove away.

She arrived at the **grocery store** first, handing a **delivery** to a Fire Element, who **rush**ed out to give her a gift. Next, she **deliver**ed a **package** to the Fire chef at a food **stall**. Then she stopped alongside a Fire couple pushing a **charcoal** grill.

Ember handed them a bottle filled with **lighter fluid**. "As ordered," she said with a smile.

The couple lifted the **lid** off the grill, revealing a **tiny** Fire baby being warmed by the **coal**s. The baby grabbed the bottle and **suck**ed it down, **burp**ing up flames.

5　**act of God** 불가항력. 신의 영역에 속하여 사람(여기에서는 원소)의 힘으로 저항할 수 없는 힘이라는 뜻으로, 이 표현을 사용해 주인공 클로드가 'God(신)' 대신에 자신의 이름 'Clod'를 넣어 말장난을 하고 있다.

"Gotta run!" said Ember. "Going for Dad's record."

The **tension** Ember felt at the shop **melt**ed away while she made deliveries. But as she pulled into **traffic** behind an old truck, she quickly lost her **patience**.

"Move it!" she hollered. She **rev**ved her scooter and **manuever**ed it around the truck. She shook her **fist**. *"Shàshà r íshà!"* she hollered. "Spark in the dirt!"

Delivery after delivery, Ember worked as quickly as she could. She placed sandbags in the arms of the owner of a smoke-cleaner shop. She handed off a **parcel** outside a woodshop. She dropped off a box of **fireworks** at a fireworks store. Fire kids standing nearby **swarm**ed around the box. The fireworks exploded to the **delight** of the kids.

But Ember didn't have time to enjoy the show. As the fireworks **lit up** the sky, she happily raced home.

When she reached the shop, a Closed sign hung on the door. Ember hurried inside and saw that the timer hadn't yet **gone off**. "Ha, ha!" she called to her father with a smile. "Winner, winner, charcoal dinner!"

But Bernie was **asleep** at the **counter**, **surround**ed by **paperwork** and red dot stickers.

Ember **toned down** her **celebration** and **tiptoe**d across the floor, trying not to wake her father. Her smile **faded** when she saw how old Bernie looked. *She* was the reason he hadn't been able to **retire**. Because she wasn't ready. Because she still **lost her temper.**

When she **drape**d a **chain mail** shawl[6] over his shoulders, Bernie woke with a **smoky cough.** Ember gently pulled a red dot sticker off his **cheek.**

"**Head** to bed," she said. "I'll close things up." She helped her father stand.

"I still have much to prepare for the Red Dot Sale," he argued.

"Dad, I'll take care of it," she insisted. "You need to rest."

Just then, the timer **rang out.** Bernie glanced at it with surprise, understanding that Ember had **beat**en his record! "How?" he asked.

Ember **shrug**ged. "I learned from the best."

They both laughed. Then Ember led her father across the shop. As they passed the Blue Flame, Bernie coughed again.

---

6   **shawl** 숄. 추위를 막거나 장식을 위해 어깨나 목 주변에 걸치는 여성용 의류.

"I am old," he said with a sigh. "I can't do this forever."
He picked up a **twig** from the **stack** at the base of the Blue
Flame's **cauldron**. "Now that you have beaten my time, there
is only one thing you haven't done. Tomorrow I will **sleep in**.
And I want *you* to run the shop for the Red Dot Sale."

Ember gasped. "Seriously? **By myself**?"

Bernie broke the twig in two and handed half to Ember.
"If you can do that without losing your temper," he **challenge**d
her, "it will show me you are able to take over."

Ember stood tall. "You got it, *Àshfá*," she said.

Bernie held the twig with both hands and closed his eyes.
Then he **toss**ed it into the Blue Flame.

"I won't **let** you **down**," said Ember. "I **swear**. You'll see."

Bernie **pat**ted her shoulder. "Hmm," he said. "Good
daughter."

As he **trudge**d up the stairs, Ember watched him go. Then
she did a happy dance. "Yes!" she cried out.

When she turned back to the Blue Flame, she held her stick
and closed her eyes. Before she tossed the stick into the cauldron,
she **whisper**ed, "Blue Flame, please let this **go my way**."

Chapter 4

Early the next morning, the streets of Firetown were calm. But inside Bernie's shop, Ember was hard at work, **slap**ping stickers onto various items.

When it was time to open, she **adjust**ed the Red Dot Sale pin on her **apron**. "Take a breath," she **remind**ed herself. "Calm as a **candle**."

When she rolled up the shade[1] on the window, a crowd of customers was waiting, but Ember **kept her cool**. She smiled and opened the door.

---

1 **shade** 햇빛 가리개. '블라인드(blind)'라고도 불리며, 창문에 달아 햇빛을 가리는 물건. 주로 천이나 목재, 플라스틱판 등을 연결하여 늘어뜨린 것으로, 상하로 작동하여 햇빛의 양을 조절한다.

"Morning," she said. "Welcome to the Fireplace—"

Before she could finish, customers **rush**ed in, **practically trampling** her **flame**s.

One customer headed toward some cans **arrange**d in a pyramid.[2] Instead of taking the top can, the customer **yank**ed one out from the bottom. As the stack **wobble**d, Ember hurried over.

"Whoa, whoa!" she cried. "They're all the same. Just take one from the top." She handed a can to the customer. "Thanks for shopping!"

Another customer **heave**d an **armload** of red stickers onto the counter. "So many stickers for sale!" the customer **grunt**ed.

"Are these **fragile**?" asked another customer as they **swept** a **shelf** of **delicate** items into their basket.

"No, wait!" cried Ember—too late.

Smash! Several **shatter**ed on the floor.

Ember **stifle**d a **yell**. She tried to calm herself and keep her cool. Then she saw another customer about to put a **log**

---

2 **pyramid** 피라미드. 고대 이집트의 왕이나 왕족 무덤의 한 형식으로, 돌이나 벽돌을 쌓아 만든 사각뿔 모양의 거대한 건축물.

in their mouth—without even paying! "You have to pay before you eat," she reminded them, yanking the log away.

The morning passed by in a **blur**. Amid the **endless stream** of customers and the **constant** *ring* of the **cash register**, Ember tried to stay calm. Her father was **count**ing **on** her. But the customers had so many questions!

"Does this come in a large?"

"What's your return **policy**?"

"Has anyone seen my husband?"

Ember's flames turned bright red. *Take a breath,* she reminded herself.

"My dad broke this," said a Fire child, holding up a **damage**d toy.

Make **connection**, Ember told herself through **grit**ted teeth.

"Mind if I test this **kettle**?" asked a customer, just as the kettle **release**d a **high-pitched whistle**.

Ember was about to **blow her top**, too. It was all too much.

She **strain**ed to keep her cool. But any moment now, she'd blow. She could almost *feel* her flames turning purple.

"Back in five minutes!" Ember **choke**d **out** through gritted teeth.

She rushed from the room, her hand **clamp**ed over her mouth and **sparks** flying. She **made it** down the **basement** steps. Then she **let out** a **fiery blast**. "Ahhhhhh!"

As the smoke **clear**ed, Ember **pant**ed, trying to **recover**. That was when a pipe in the basement began to **vibrate**.

The pipe **groan**ed, **squeal**ed, and then . . . **crack**ed. *Whoosh!* It shot a stream of water straight at Ember.

Ouch![3] She **duck**ed as it **douse**d part of her flame.

More water **gush**ed from the pipe, quickly **flood**ing the floor. Ember **gasp**ed when the **brick** support **column** in the middle of the basement **shudder**ed.

As water continued to fill the basement, Ember **dodge**d the painful **spray**. She had to do something before the situation got even worse. Thinking fast, she grabbed a trash can **lid** and a fireplace poker.[4] She climbed onto some **float**ing **debris** and then reached toward the cracked pipe.

Water stung her flames as she pushed the lid against the

---

3   ouch '아야!'라는 뜻으로, 갑자기 아픔을 느낄 때 나오는 소리.
4   poker 부지깽이. 아궁이에 불을 땔 때 연료가 잘 탈 수 있도록 들추거나 밀어 넣는 데 쓰는 가늘고 긴 막대기.

broken pipe, stopping the spray. She melted the poker in her hand and used it to **weld** the **edge**s of the lid against the pipe. Then she **held her breath** and released her **grip**.

The lid **stay**ed **put**. The water stopped!

But as Ember glanced around the **water-logged** basement, she began to **panic**. "Oh, no. Stupid temper. Not today!"

Her own flame was damaged, too. She grabbed a few sticks from a shelf and ate them, **replenish**ing her flame. "What is wrong with me?" she cried.

A picture frame floated on the water. When it began to move, Ember **suck**ed in her breath. Two streams of water **fountain**ed up out of the pool and two watery hands appeared, holding the frame. Then Wade Ripple, a young Water man, sat up. He was **bawl**ing his eyes out!

Ember gasped. "What the . . . ?" she said.

Wade studied the picture in the frame and cried some more. "What a happy family," he said, **sniffling**. "Is that you and your *dad*?" He pointed at the picture of Ember sitting on her father's **lap**, blowing out birthday candles. "I love dads. And it's your birthday!" He cried so hard now, his tears **splash**ed Ember.

She **winced**, **shield**ing her face. "Who are you?" she **demand**ed. "What are you doing here?"

"I don't know!" Wade **sob**bed. "I was searching for a **leak** on the other side of the river and got sucked in. This is bad! I can't lose another job! I just can't seem to find my flow."

When he stood, Ember couldn't help noticing that he was tall and *very* **muscular**. "Dang,[5]" she **whisper**ed. Her flames burned pink.

Wade glanced down. "Ugh, that pipe **squish**ed me all **out of shape**," he said. He shook his body until the muscles **disappear**ed and his **belly plop**ped back out. "That's better."

"Dude,[6] just get out of here," Ember **plead**ed, growing **impatient** now. "I gotta clean this **mess** before my dad sees what I did."

Wade stopped crying and **straighten**ed up. "Oh, actually . . . ," he said, **slosh**ing toward the other side of the room. He grabbed a pen and notepad from under his shirt. "I'm afraid I'm going to have to write you a **ticket**."

---

5 **dang** '이런', '젠장'이라는 뜻으로 못마땅함이나 짜증스러움 등을 나타내는 속어인 'damn'을 완곡하게 말하는 표현이다.

6 **dude** 젊은 남자를 가리키는 속어.

"A ticket?" cried Ember.

"Yeah, I'm a city **inspector**," said Wade. "And this pipe is **definitely** not **up to code**."

Ember held her face with her hands. "I sucked a city inspector into our pipes?"

"I know—**ironic**, right?" said Wade. He **poke**d at the pipe, which **rumbled**.

"Stop messing with that!" cried Ember.

"I need to make sure it's **solid**," Wade explained.

"It's solid," Ember **confirm**ed. "I should know. My dad built it himself."

"Wait," said Wade, glancing up. "Your dad did?"

"Yes! **With his bare hands**," said Ember with **pride**. "Every brick and board. This place was a **ruin** when he found it."

"Wow, he did all of this himself?" asked Wade. "Without **permit**s?" He began to **weep** again.

Ember **gulp**ed. "Uh . . ."

"I'm gonna have to write that up, too," said Wade. "First I'm sucked into a pipe, and now I have to write **citation**s that could get this place **shut down**. Oh gosh, it's just too much!" Tears streamed from his eyes.

Ember **flare**d up. "Shut us *down*?"

"I know!" **wail**ed Wade. "It's **awful!**"

"No! You can't shut us down," Ember **beg**ged. "Please! This is a big day for me. It's our Red Dot Sale!" She **lunge**d for Wade's notepad.

"Hey, **take it easy**," he said, flowing out of her path. "This is as hard on me as it is on you." He **scribble**d **furiously** on his pad. He sloshed toward the basement window.

"Get back here!" cried Ember.

"Sorry," said Wade. "I gotta get these to **City Hall** before the end of my **shift**." Without another word, he **pour**ed his body through the high, narrow window and disappeared.

Ember was right behind him. She **rip**ped off her apron. Then she **blaze**d through the window and **chase**d after Wade. "Get back here!"

At that moment, a pipe **joint** began to leak.

But Ember didn't notice.

Chapter 5

From the shop, Bernie glanced through the window—just in time to see Ember **chasing** a Water man down the street. "Hmm?" Bernie asked **aloud**.

Ember followed Wade toward the Wetro station and the bridge that she had told Clod would take an act of God for her to cross. But as Wade **board**ed a train, Ember knew she had to follow.

"Next stop, **Element** City!" the **announcer**'s voice **rang out**.

As the doors of the last train car started to close, Ember pulled her hood[1] over her flames and stepped inside.

She **scan**ned the crowd for Wade. Ember tried to **squeeze** past a huge, **grassy** Earth Element, but when the train **lurch**ed, she **accidentally slam**med into the Earth man.

Poof! His grass burned up, leaving a very **skinny** guy. "Hay!**2**" he cried.

"Sorry!" said Ember.

Then she **spot**ted Wade ahead. The train car was too **crowded** for her to squeeze through. Thinking fast, she climbed out a window.

As Ember **inch**ed along the outside of the car, wind **whip**ped her flames. Then Ember saw water **splash** from an **aqueduct** ahead. The train was about to pass under a giant **waterfall**!

She gasped and melted her way in through a window—just **in time**. She fell to the floor, trying to **catch her breath**.

The train car turned **pitch black** as it **barrel**ed through a tunnel.**3** Ember was the only light **source** in the train. As she

---

1 **hood** 후드. 머리 전체를 덮는 쓰개를 가리키는 말로, 주로 비옷이나 방한복에 달려 있어 비가 올 때 혹은 추울 때 머리를 덮는 데 사용한다.

2 **hay** 원래는 말린 풀을 가리키는 '건초'라는 뜻이지만, '이봐'하고 상대방을 부르는 'hey'와 발음이 같다는 점을 활용해, 여기에서는 주인공 앰버를 비격식적으로 부르는 호칭으로 쓰였다.

3 **tunnel** 터널. 철도나 도로 등을 통하게 하기 위해서 산이나 바다, 강 밑을 뚫어 만든 굴 형태의 통로.

blazed through the car, searching for Wade, other **passenger**s turned in surprise.

Suddenly, Ember saw a flame **hover**ing in front of her. **Puzzled**, she reached her hand toward the flames. "Huh? What the . . . ?"

That was when the train **burst** out of the tunnel. As light **flood**ed the train car, Ember saw that the other Fire Element was her own **reflection flicker**ing at the back of Wade's head!

Wade held a thick stack of **ticket**s in his hand—tickets that could **shut down** Bernie's shop. As Ember reached for them, Wade's hand boiled at her heat.

"This stop, **City Hall**," announced a bored-sounding voice as the train rolled into the Wetro station.

Wade glanced down at his boiling hand. "Ah!" he cried, **whirl**ing around. "Hands off!" He **whip**ped the tickets away from Ember and raced out of the train car.

"Gah!**4**" Ember exited, too, **dodging** passengers boarding the train and **apologizing** along the way.

Wade **stream**ed easily down the crowded stairs, but Ember

---

4 gah '이런!', '맙소사!'라는 뜻으로 짜증이나 분노, 절망 등을 나타내는 표현.

struggled to follow. "Ugh," she **mutter**ed. "Stop!" As she tried to hurry, she **collide**d with other passengers.

"Stop!" she cried again, but Wade was too far away. She reached the street at the same time as an Air Element, who **float**ed into the path of a passing car. *Poof!*

When the Air Element **reform**ed, his jacket[5] was on the ground. "Aw! My new jacket," he muttered as he **drift**ed away.

Ember blazed across the street and down the sidewalk after Wade. He passed a **nursery school** bus and then streamed through a crowd of Earth kids.

The kids **block**ed Ember's path. Thinking fast, Ember popped open her umbrella and fired up her flames. Like a hot-air **balloon**, she floated high over the kids, gazing down at their **amazed** faces.

But when her umbrella melted, she **tumble**d to the ground, **land**ing on some trash cans. She pushed herself up and chased after Wade.

Wade saw Ember coming. He took a **sharp** left.

Ember **skid**ded to a stop and saw that he had **slip**ped into

---

5 **jacket** 재킷. 앞 부분이 터져 있고 소매가 달린 짧은 겉옷.

a narrow space between two buildings. She squeezed in her flames and **shimmied** after him.

They both **work**ed **their way** through the tight **passageway**.

Wade reached the **opening** on the other side, but his ticket book got caught in a **crevice**. He **grunt**ed, trying to pull it out. It finally gave way, and he splashed onto the sidewalk.

Moments later, Ember **emerged**, too. As she and Wade raced toward City Hall, she **swipe**d a bottle of **chili** oil from a dirt burger **vendor**'s cart.

"Huh?" said the vendor.

Ember blazed ahead until she was in Wade's path. She **squirt**ed the chili oil onto the sidewalk. The oil fed her flames, creating a huge wall of fire.

"Come on, guy," she said. "You can't get through this. So it is time to hand 'em over."

"Oh, boy,[6]" he said. "I'm sorry. This is going to be really **disappointing** for you."

He sloshed forward and poured down through a **nearby** sidewalk **grate**. Then he **spout**ed up through another grate

---

6   **boy** 여기에서는 '소년'이라는 뜻이 아니라, '맙소사' 또는 '어머나'라는 의미로 놀람이나 실망, 기쁨 등을 나타내는 표현으로 쓰였다.

past Ember. He gave her one last look as she watched him step into the **revolving door**s of City Hall.

"No, no, no, no, no, no!" cried Ember.

"Sorry!" called Wade.

Ember's flame **dim**med with **despair**. "Please! No!" she **holler**ed after him. "You don't understand."

As her shoulders **slump**ed, her **inner prismatic** light **glow**ed like a sad, **weary** rainbow.

Inside the building, Wade placed his tickets in a **canister**. He **load**ed the canister into a **vacuum** tube and **let** it **go**. *Foomp!* Then he noticed **fleck**s of colorful light dancing across the wall.

"Whoa," said Wade. He glanced out the window to find the source of the light.

It was Ember, just outside the door. "The shop is my dad's dream," she was saying, more to herself than to him. "If I'm the reason it gets shut down, it will kill him. He will never trust me to **take over**."

"Aw," Wade **murmur**ed. He held a hand to his **chest**, his face covered in tears, and stepped outside.

"Why didn't you say that before?" he asked Ember.

She zipped up her fire, **shield** on. "Wait, does that mean you'll **tear** up the tickets?" she asked.

"I mean, I would," said Wade. "But I just sent them over to the **processing department**." He **gesture**d toward the vacuum tube system inside the doors.

Ember **growl**ed and held her head in **frustration**.

Wade spoke quickly. "But I can take you there so you can **plead** your case!"

Ember **perk**ed **up**, hope flickering in her chest.

Chapter 6

Ember followed Wade into an office filled with **tangled**, **leafy** **vines**. She could **barely** see through the **thick** jungle of **stalks** and leaves. When Wade pushed past a **branch**, it **snap**ped back at Ember.

"Whoa!" she cried, **duck**ing.

At the back of the office, a large **Earth** guy sat at a **cluttered** desk with a **nameplate** that read FERN GROUCHWOOD. His **overgrown** leaves **sprout**ed this way and that. Only his **grassy mustache** appeared **tidy** and **trim**med.

"Hey, Fern!" said Wade with a bright smile. "How you doing?"

"Living the dream," **mumble**d Fern. On the **tree-stump** desk before him, his **inbox overflow**ed with papers. Behind him, **vacuum** tubes lined the wall.

Wade laughed **nervously**. "You know those **citation**s I just sent you from Firetown?"

Fern held up a metal **canister** filled with forms. "I was about to send them to Mrs. Cumulus," he said slowly, "then get sprayed for fungus[1] **rot**." He started to put the canister into a tube.

"Wait!" cried Ember.

Fern **hesitate**d.

"Before you do," said Wade, "maybe she could **have a word**?" He **nod**ded to Ember.

She **lean**ed across the desk toward Fern. "Hi . . . ," she began with a smile. But then . . . *hiss!* Her hot hands **singe**d the wooden desk, leaving **handprint**s. "Whoa!" she cried, stepping backward.

Fern **stare**d at her, **unamused**.

Ember tried to sound bright and **breezy**. "Look, I know

---

1 **fungus** 곰팡이류. 가는 실 모양의 세포를 가진 균으로, 생물에 여러가지 질병을 일으키기도 하지만 유익한 것도 많다. 엽록소가 없어 광합성을 하지 않으며 어둡고 습한 곳에서 자란다.

that we have some non-**permit**ted stuff in our shop," she said. She **wink**ed at the word *non-permitted*. "But who doesn't **skate around** permits sometimes?" She laughed and raised her hand. "**Guilty**."

Fern didn't even **crack a smile**. "You **realize** you're saying this, **out loud**, to the actual permit office, right?" He started again to put the canister into the tube.

"Wait!" cried Ember and Wade at the **exact** same time.

"Tell him what you told me, about your dad and **let**ting him **down**," said Wade quickly.

"No!" snapped Ember, **flaring** up. "That's **personal**!"

Wade leaned backward, away from her hot flames. "It really **got to** me. He might feel it, too." He started to tell the story himself. "Her dad will be super—" he began.

"Nope!" Ember tried to cover his mouth.

But Wade kept talking. "Super—"

"Nope!" said Ember again. She searched for something to **stuff** into Wade's face.

"Super **disa**—" he said.

Ember **grab**bed the nameplate from Fern's desk and **shove**d it into Wade's mouth. It floated, **suspend**ed, in his watery face, but he kept talking.

"—ppointed in her," he somehow managed to say.

Ember's heat rose. She **took a** deep **breath** and blew it out in short bursts, trying to calm herself. Then she pleaded with Wade. "Stop it!"

He wouldn't stop talking to Fern, even with the nameplate in his mouth. "He might even be . . ."

Ember reached for a snow globe[2] from Fern's desk and shoved it into Wade's face, **knock**ing out the nameplate.

His mouth was full now, but Wade **eked out** one more word: ". . . **ashamed**."

Ember continued her stress-breathing,[3] but it wasn't working. "What are you doing?" She felt her flames start to turn purple.

"But the main thing is if her father can't **retire**," said Wade, who was **weep**ing now, "it will be all Ember's . . . f-f-f—"

---

2 **snow globe** 스노 글로브. 흔들면 마치 눈이 내리는 듯한 풍경이 연출되는 데서 비롯된 명칭으로, 투명한 액체로 채워진 구(球) 모양의 유리 안에 축소 모형을 넣어 만든 장식품. 우리나라에서는 '스노볼(snowball)'이라고도 불린다.

3 **stress-breathing** 심리적 또는 신체적 긴장 상태에 있을 때 몸과 마음이 편안해질 수 있도록 돕는 호흡법.

Fern **hung on Wade's every word** now, waiting.

But before Wade could finish his sentence, Ember **explode**d in a ball of fire. "STOP TALKING!" she **roar**ed.

When the smoke **clear**ed, Fern's hair was singed black and his grass mustache was gone. His burned wire-**rimmed** glasses sat **askew** on his nose. Everything on Fern's desk had **burn**ed **to a crisp**, too—except the citations that would shut down Bernie's shop. Those were inside a metal canister.

Wade **douse**d a **flaming** bobblehead[4] on the desk as Fern studied his **scorched** inbox. "Looks like I'm going home early today," he said **flatly**. He put the canister into the tube.

"No, don't—" Ember **beg**ged, her flames blazing with **desperation**.

The tickets shot through the vacuum tube. *Foomp!*

"Expect to get shut down within a week," said Fern as he stood. "Have a good one.[5]"

On his way out of the office, which now looked like a scorched jungle, he handed Ember a **brochure** titled *So*

Your Business Is Being Shut Down. Ember **sigh**ed, feeling **absolutely** and **utterly defeated**.

"Sorry," whispered Wade, his eyes **teary**.

Ember slowly walked home over the bridge, all the way back to the shop. When she got there, she saw the Closed sign hanging on the door. She gasped. "What? Already?"

She burst into the shop.

"Hello?"

When Ember heard her father **cough**ing in the basement, she rushed down the stairs. She couldn't believe what she was seeing. Pipes had **burst** and were **leak**ing everywhere! Her parents were **desperately** trying to clean up the **mess**.

"Oh no," Ember said. "Dad! What happened?" she asked.

"We are lucky nobody got hurt," Bernie said in a rush. "It *ruined* the Red Dot Sale!"

Ember **winced** with **guilt**.

"Did *he* do this?" Bernie cried.

"Who?" asked Ember.

"That Water guy I saw you **chase**." Water **drip**ped onto

Bernie's face from above. He **cringe**d at the **sting**.

"Oh, uh, um . . . yeah, he did," Ember **fib**bed. "He just broke through a pipe. I don't know why. Luckily, I was able to close it off. I, uh, couldn't catch him, though."

Bernie flared with anger. "Water," he **spat**. "Always trying to **water** us **down**!"

"He was a Water *person*, Dad, not just water," she reminded Bernie.

"Same thing," he **grumble**d. "And why is there water in the pipes? The city shut it down years ago. There should be *no water*!" He coughed again, so **violently** that he nearly fell backward.

"Dad!" Ember caught him just before he hit the water.

"Bernie!" Cinder cried out. She led him toward the stairs and **rub**bed his back. "We will **get through** this. Just like before."

"Before?" asked Ember.

Cinder **sank** to the step beside Bernie. "There is a reason we left Fire Land," she said. "Oh, Ember, it was so beautiful there." She smiled at the memory.

"Here in Firetown, we are the only family with a Blue

Flame. But back home, *every* family had one." Cinder described the Blue Flames in the windows, **including** the one in the restaurant Bernie and Cinder had started in Fire Land. Cinder had been **pregnant** with Ember then.

"Your father put everything we had into starting our life together. But then a great storm came," Cinder said, her voice **grave**.

She described how she and Bernie had looked up and seen a storm **brew**ing above the **rooftop**s. Then the **ferocious** winds had hit.

Debris crashed down inside the restaurant, knocking over the **cauldron** with the Blue Flame. Bernie had acted quickly, **capturing** the Flame in a lantern as the restaurant continued to **collapse**.

"All was lost for us," said Cinder.

After the storm, the restaurant was a **pile** of **rubble**. Most of the neighbors' buildings had been **damage**d, too. "But it was too painful to stay," said Cinder. "We needed to start over, somewhere new."

And so they boarded a boat they had found on the beach. Bernie's parents watched as the boat pulled away from the

shore. "It was the last time your father ever saw his family," said Cinder, her voice heavy. "That is why we came here. To build this. Our new life."

Bernie was **mop**ping the floor now, but he listened with tears in his eyes. Ember had never seen him so **emotional**. She looked at the brochure from Fern and felt her fire **reignite**.

"*Àshfá*, nothing will happen to this shop or the flame again," Ember **vow**ed. "I promise."

Bernie touched Ember's **cheek** and smiled **wearily**. "Good daughter," he murmured.

Chapter 7

The next morning, Wade **head**ed to work at **City Hall**. Music from his headphones **vibrate**d throughout his watery head. He **approach**ed the door to his **department**. He was so into his music that he didn't see the **flame**s burning on the floor—until his bag caught fire.

Wade **glance**d down. "Ah! Fire. Fire!" He **desperately pat**ted at his burning bag. "Ah! Fire!" He **stomp**ed on the flames that rose from the floor.

Suddenly, Ember stood up, her body forming from the flames. "Hey. Hey!" she cried until Wade stopped stomping on her.

"Oh, sorry!" he said, stepping back. "You're so hot!" He checked his **smolder**ing bag.

Ember raised an **eyebrow**. "Excuse me?"

"No!" he said quickly. "I mean, like you're smokin'[1]! No, I didn't mean it like tha—"

"Are you done yet?" asked Ember.

Wade dripped with **embarrassment**. "Yes, please."

"I'm waiting to talk to your **boss**," she explained. "So make like a stream and . . . flow somewhere else." She **settle**d back on the floor, ready to wait.

"Actually," said Wade, "Gale won't be in today. She's a *huge* airball fan, and the Windbreakers are finally in the playoffs![2] *Toot, toot!*" He **pump**ed his **fist**.

Ember flared with **frustration**. "Ugh!"

Wade leaned away from her heat. "Okay . . . well, I just **came by** because I left my **pass**es for the game here last night."

Ember **perk**ed **up**. "Passes?" she asked, standing tall.

---

1 **smokin'** 'smoking hot'의 줄임말로, '매력적인', '멋진'이라는 뜻의 속어.

2 **playoff** 플레이오프. 농구나 야구와 같은 스포츠에서 정규 리그를 끝낸 다음, 최종 우승 팀을 가리기 위해 별도로 치르는 경기.

"Like, **plural**?"

Things were **look**ing **up**. . . .

A short while later, Ember and Wade hurried up the Wetro station stairs into the busy Air **District**. Ember stared in **awe** at the **throng** of Airball fans floating into Cyclone[3] **Stadium**. The stadium was tall and **cylindrical**, like a cyclone. The **marquee** read WINDBREAKERS VS. CROP DUSTERS.

The game had already begun inside the stadium as Wade and Ember **made their way** toward Gale.

High above the **stand**s, **fluffy** Air players dressed in jerseys[4] passed a ball toward a **hoop**.

Ember couldn't help watching the exciting game. Then she remembered why they had come—to find Gale. "Where is she?" she asked, **scan**ning the stadium.

"Up there," Wade said, gesturing. "In that skybox.[5]"

3 **cyclone** 사이클론. 적도 부근의 열대 해상에서 발생하는 열대성 저기압으로, 강한 바람과 폭풍우를 일으켜 막대한 피해를 입힌다. 여기에서는 '사이클론'이 공기 구역에 있는 경기장 이름으로 쓰였다.

4 **jersey** 저지. 운동선수들이 경기할 때 입는 옷. 보통 숫자가 적혀 있으며, 앞쪽에는 팀 명칭이 있고 뒤쪽에는 선수의 이름이 쓰여 있다.

5 **skybox** 스카이 박스. 스포츠 경기장의 높은 곳에 일반 관람석과 별도로 만들어 놓은 고급 관람 시설.

The Air woman in the skybox **swell**ed like a purple storm cloud. "Come on!" she **bellow**ed at the players and refs.[6]

Fear **flicker**ed in Ember's **chest**, but only for a moment. "Okay," she said, taking a deep breath. "Time to cancel some tickets."

As she made her way toward the skybox, she passed a drink **vendor**. "Toot-toot juice!" they called. "Getcha toot-toot juice!"

When Ember reached the **row** of seats behind Gale's box, she stopped. A few Water Elements sat between her and Gale. They would likely boil if she passed by them. Cyclone Stadium was yet another part of Element City that had *not* been built with Fire Elements in mind.

"You'll be great!" **encourage**d Wade. "This way." He started down the row.

Ember **suck**ed in her flames and followed. "Excuse me. Sorry. Pardon. Oh, sorry," she said. "Fire girl coming through."

"Jimmy, what's up?" Wade called to a fan. "Wendy!" he **greet**ed another. "How good is it to be here?" Wade seemed

---

6 ref 'referee(심판)'의 줄임말.

to know everyone.

But Ember wasn't making any friends. The Water Elements boiled as she passed.

Finally, she and Wade took their seats behind Gale. "Break some wind!" Gale **thunder**ed at the players.

"Hi, Gale!" called Wade. "How you doing?"

Gale glanced back at him. "Look at the **score**," she **rumble**d. "What do you think?" Then she **blast**ed the players again. "Blow the *ball,* not the game!"

Ember found the **courage** to speak. "Yeah, so uh, Gale, my name is Ember Lumen. My family runs a Fire shop. . . . Wade wrote us a **bunch** of **ticket**s yesterday, and—"

Buzz!

Gale grew even stormier. "What kind of **call** was that?" she cried at the referee. Then she turned **impatiently** toward Ember. "Lumen? Yeah, Fire shop with thirty **citation**s . . ."

Ember **shot** Wade a look. "Thirty!"

He **shrug**ged and gave a nervous laugh.

Ember turned back to Gale. "Anyway, friend, I was hoping we could **work** something **out**—"

As the buzzer sounded again, she thundered at the ref.

"Come on, ref! Are your eyes in the back of your head?"

On the field above, the Air ref's eyes **rotate**d to the back of his **puffy** head and he **glare**d at Gale. As the crowd **boo**ed, Gale's cloud **darken**ed.

"Oh, no," warned Wade, as if he knew what was coming.

Ember did *not* see what was coming. She tried again. "Yeah, **bummer**," she said to Gale. "Okay, so the thirty citations—"

"Do you mind?" Gale thundered. "There's a *game* going on." She **whirl**ed back around and muttered under her breath, *"Fireball."*

Ember couldn't believe her ears. Her flames flickered. "Fireball?" she **repeat**ed. She stood and stepped in front of Gale, **block**ing her view.

"Actually," said Ember, "I do mind. This is my *life* we're talking about, not just some game."

Gale swelled like a thundercloud.[7] "Some game?" she repeated, her lightning **flash**ing. "This is the *playoffs*. So forgive me if I don't want to hear a **sob** story about the

---

7   **thundercloud** 뇌운. 천둥과 번개를 동반한 소나기를 내리는 구름.

problems of some little shop."

Ember's flames shot higher, **streak**ed **ominously** with purple. "Well, that 'little shop' matters *way* more than a bunch of **overpaid** cloud **puff**s blowing some ball around."

Gale **loom**ed over Ember, leaning forward until they were nose to nose. "I **dare** you," Gale bellowed. "Say 'cloud puffs' one . . . more . . . time."

Ember didn't back down. "Cloud," she said. *"Puffs."* She stood so close to Gale that her hot words blew away Gale's nose.

Furious, Gale **reform**ed her nose. As the crowd booed, Wade checked the game. "Oh, no!" he murmured.

Gale looked, too, and **gasp**ed.

"Huh?" said Ember.

"Lutz!" cried Wade.

He gestured toward one of the Windbreakers, who **race**d to **guard** the net just as a Crop Duster player blew forward with the ball. *Whoosh!* The ball blew right through Lutz's cloud, straight into the net.

As the crowd booed, Lutz's **spirit sank**.

"Lutz man," said Wade. "He's been in such a **funk** 'cause

his mom has been sick."

As if to **prove** Wade's point, an **opponent** stole the ball from Lutz. Boos rose from the **agitated** Windbreaker fans.

"That is so not cool," said Wade, **survey**ing the crowd. "He's doing his best."

Wade suddenly stood and shouted **skyward**. "We love you, Lutz!" He gestured for other fans to join the **chant**. "We love you, Lutz! We love you, Lutz! C'mon! We love you, Lutz! Everybody!"

The crowd responded. Soon the chant rose from the stands. "We love you, Lutz! We love you, Lutz!"

Lutz glanced at the **cheer**ing **section** and smiled.

By now, the whole stadium had **pick**ed **up** the cheer. Then Wade started doing the wave.[8] *"Whoooaaa . . ."* he cried as he **ripple**d his watery body up and down.

Every Water Element in the stands **follow**ed **suit**. A tidal wave[9] of Water Elements rolled around the stadium. When

---

8   **wave** 파도타기 응원. 운동 경기를 관람하는 관중들이 시작점을 정해서 차례대로 손을 머리 위로 들며 일어섰다 앉았다를 반복해, 마치 파도가 출렁이는 듯한 모양을 만들어 경기에 호응하고 선수 들을 응원하는 방식.

9   **tidal wave** 해일. 폭풍이나 지진, 화산 폭발 등에 의하여 바닷물이 갑자기 비정상적으로 높아져 육지로 넘쳐 들어오는 현상.

it made its way back to Ember, she opened her umbrella to **shield** herself from the splash.

On the court, Lutz was **energized**. He **slam**med the ball into the net. Score!

The crowd **leap**ed to their feet. Even Ember got caught up in the moment. "Ah, yes!" she cheered. "Yes!"

"Woo!" cried Wade, tearing up with emotion. "**Way to go**, Lutz!"

Lutz raised his fluffy arms in victory.

As Wade continued to cheer for Lutz, Ember stared at Wade for a moment. *He* was pretty amazing, too. He had **inspire**d the whole crowd to support Lutz, which had turned the **tide** of the game.

When fans started high-fiving,[10] Wade laughed and joined in. "Uh! Yeah!" he said, **slap**ping his watery **palm** against theirs. "Woo-hoo!"

But when he tried to high-five Ember, she raised an eyebrow. Fire and water were a danger to each other. What **awful** things might happen if they touched?

---

10 high-five 하이파이브. 승리나 성공을 기뻐하기 위해 두 사람이 동시에 한 손을 들어 손바닥을 마주치는 행동.

"Oh," Wade said, **lower**ing his arm.

He reached over and gave himself an **awkward** high five with his other hand. *Smack!*

Chapter 8

After the game, **rowdy** fans **pour**ed out of the **stadium**. Drums **pound**ed out a victory song while fans cheered and laughed.

"Woo-hoo!" cried Gale. "What a comeback!"

"Check out who found the gift shop!" called Wade. He was covered **head to toe** in Windbreakers **gear**. He waved a foam hand[1] and shouted, "Woo!"

Ember **grin**ned. "I gotta **admit**," she said to Gale, "that *was* pretty cool."

"You can see why I can get all **churn**ed up," said Gale.

---

1 **foam hand** 스포츠에서 특정 팀을 응원하는 용도로 손에 착용하는 커다란 손가락 모양의 응원 도구.

"But as a 'cloud **puff**' who used to come here with her dad, these wins mean a little bit more."

"And as a 'fireball' who's supposed to **take over** her dad's shop . . . ," began Ember. She hesitated. The words weren't easy to say **out loud**. "I sure don't want to **let** him **down**. And I could use a win, too."

Wade saw Ember's soft, colorful light shine through. She was finally **let**ting **her guard down**.

"Now I just gotta stop the water from coming in—" she continued.

"*Water?* In *Firetown?*" said Gale.

"Yeah?" said Ember, **confused**.

"Water was **shut off** to there *years* ago," said Gale. "Forget the **ticket**s. I'm gonna have to **take apart** your dad's shop to **figure out** what's going on!"

"You can't!" cried Ember. "My dad put his *whole life* into that place!"

"*Argh*," Gale grumbled to Wade. "I **bet** this is connected to that **fluff**in'**2** leak."

---

2 fluffin' 동사 'fluff'는 '망치다', '부풀리다'라는 두 가지 뜻이 있다. 여기에서는 두 가지 뜻 모두에 착안하여, 공기 종족의 몹시 짜증스러운 감정을 강조하는 표현으로 쓰였다.

Wade explained to Ember, "We've been trying to **track down** a leak in the city. It's why I was in the **canal** and— Wait!" He whirled around to face Gale. "I know where I got sucked into Ember's shop! Ember and I could **track** the water from her shop and find the **source** of the leak!"

Gale looked **intrigued**. "Keep talking," she said.

"I could call in a city **crew** to fix whatever we find," Wade said.

Ember **jump**ed **on board**. "Yes!" she cried. "And there'd be no need to touch my dad's shop!"

Gale churned that over, then smiled at their **hopeful** faces. "You're lucky you're a cute couple," she said.

Ember's cheeks burned. "Oh, we're not a—" she said quickly.

Gale **cut** her **off**. "You got until Friday. If you can find the leak and get a crew to fix it by then, those tickets are forgiven. If not? Your dad's shop gets **shut down**." With those last words, Gale **drift**ed off to join the flow of cheering fans.

"Thank you!" Ember called. She looked at Wade, who was still wearing *way* too much fan gear. "Please take all that off," she said.

"But I got you a hat!" he cried, **plunk**ing a Windbreakers hat onto Ember's head.

Poof! It **instantly** burned up.

"Okay," said Wade.

That night, Ember and Wade stood outside Bernie's shop, where Bernie wouldn't see them. Ember knew her father wasn't a fan of Water **Element**s. But she needed to work with Wade to track down the source of the leak.

"Just keep outta **sight**, okay?" asked Ember. "It'd be a whole thing."

Just then, Bernie's voice bellowed from above. "Now there's water upstairs?" he cried.

Ember and Wade **peek**ed through the shop window. Bernie had **rip**ped a piece of plaster[3] from the wall, **reveal**ing another **leaky** pipe. "It's in the walls," he **groan**ed. "I don't understand! I fix one pipe and another one leaks!"

Bernie **rush**ed to move the Blue Flame out of harm's way.

---

3 **plaster** 플라스터. 석고에 톱밥 등을 섞어 만든 건축 재료. 마르면 단단해지는 성질을 이용하여 주로 벽이나 천장을 마감하는 데 널리 쓰인다.

"Ah, water!" he grumbled as the leaky pipe **spray**ed water across the room.

Bernie threw open the window. As smoke **billow**ed out from his wet flames, he began coughing. Ember and Wade pressed themselves to the wall so he wouldn't see them.

When Bernie left the window, Ember **whisper**ed to Wade, "How could it be worse?"

"Now that water's back, the **pressure** is forcing it up to *all* your pipes," Wade explained.

"We gotta find the source!" replied Ember. She and Wade **crouch**ed down to look through the **basement** window, and then at a pipe that led from the shop to the **culvert** and into the floor of the canal near her house.

"How did you even **end up** here?" Ember asked.

Wade **recall**ed the moment clearly. "Well, I was in the canals, checking the doors for leaks . . . when I found some water that shouldn't have been there." He had **dip**ped his finger in the **puddle** and tasted it. It was **rusty**, with a **hint** of motor oil.[4]

---

4 **motor oil** 엔진 오일. 기계 부품의 마찰과 마모 현상을 줄이고, 과열을 방지하기 위해 엔진 내부에 넣는 윤활유.

Suddenly, a rush of water had **knock**ed Wade off his feet. Then he got sucked into a filtering system. Then, *bam!* He'd gotten **jam**med into a pipe that was **clog**ged with debris.

"But then I heard this **explosion** . . ." Wade described the **vibration** that had shaken the pipe, breaking up the debris. He had **burst** out and come **face to face** with Ember. "That's how I ended up at your place."

Ember sighed. She knew the **exact** source of the "explosion" Wade had heard. "Oh, flame, my temper caused this?" Ember **gaze**d at all the canals **in the distance**. "So we're searching for water 'somewhere' in a canal?" she groaned. "Those canals go *everywhere*."

Wade agreed. "It's why tracking down that leak has been so dang hard."

Ember **simmer**ed over this, trying to think of a plan. Then she glanced upward.

"The roof!" Ember said suddenly. It would give them a *much* better view.

Chapter 9

From the **rooftop** of Bernie's shop, Ember and Wade looked out over the canals. But to get an even better view, Ember knew they needed to be higher.

She **slid** a tarp[1] off part of the **chimney**, which was **top**ped with a smoke cap. When she **melt**ed the smoke cap[2] off its stand, it **toppled**, nearly hitting Wade. He **yelp**ed and **dart**ed out of the way.

Ember tied the tarp to the **upside-down** smoke cap. "You

---

1 **tarp** 방수포. 물이나 다른 액체가 통과하지 못하도록 특수 처리를 한 천.
2 **smoke cap** 굴뚝 위에 설치하는 장치로, 비와 바람을 막아 연기가 역류하는 것을 막고 원활하게 연기가 배출될 수 있도록 도와 준다.

might want to step back," she warned. Then she threw the tarp high over her head and blew flames into it. The tarp **inflate**d. Ember had made a **makeshift** hot-air **balloon**!

Wade gazed up in **astonishment**. "Holy dewdrop!³" he **exclaim**ed.

"Shh!" said Ember, hoping her father wouldn't hear. "Get in."

Wade climbed into the smoke-cap basket of the "balloon." As it rose into the air, he **stare**d at Ember with wonder. Her beautiful **blaze** shone bright, and he was so close to her now, he could feel her heat. When his arm started to boil, he **reluctantly lean**ed away.

As they **float**ed above Firetown, Wade **recognize**d the **spot** where he'd gotten sucked into the pipes. He pointed toward a puddle, one of many that led up that canal. "More water. Go that way!"

Ember **steer**ed the balloon. As they passed the **darken**ed window of a tall building, her light **illuminate**d two **Earth**

---

3   **holy dewdrop** '이런!', '세상에!'라는 뜻으로 놀라움을 나타내는 표현. 영미권에서는 'holy' 뒤에 다른 말을 추가해서 감탄사로 사용하는데, 여기에서 물의 종족인 웨이드는 'dewdrop(이슬 방울)'이 라는 말을 덧붙였다.

Elements inside who were picking each other's fruit. They **froze**.

"Nothing **weird** going on here," called one.

"Uh, just a little **pruning**," said the other.

Wade and Ember shared a laugh, and then fell into an **awkward silence** as they floated away from the window.

"So, uh, what do you do at the shop, if you don't mind me asking?" **inquire**d Wade.

"My dad's **retiring**," Ember explained, "and I'll be **taking over**. Someday, when I'm ready."

"It must be nice knowing what you're gonna do," said Wade. "After my dad **pass**ed, I got all 'What's the **point**?' Now I just go from one job to the next."

Ember gazed into the darkness. "There's a word in Firish," she said. "*Tìshók*'. It means **embrace** the light while it burns, 'cause it won't always last forever."

"Tee-shook . . . ," Wade said carefully, trying to **accurately repeat** the word.

Ember hid a smile. "Or something like that," she said.

As the balloon rounded a large building, the main part of Element City came into view. Ember spotted a familiar building and her shoulders **slump**ed.

"You okay?" Wade asked.

"Yeah," she **fib**bed.

"You sure?" asked Wade.

Ember glanced downward. "It's just . . . that building over there?" She pointed. "That's Garden Central Station."

Ember began to recall a **childhood** memory. "When I was a kid, my dad took me there because they had a Vivisteria tree. I'd always wanted to see one. It's the only flower that can **thrive** in *any* **environment**. Fire **included**."

Ember remembered the sign **advertising** the **bloom**ing Vivisteria. She had **grab**bed her father's hand and run toward the station. But as they'd approached the **entrance**, a **guard** had stopped them.

"I was so excited," Ember **murmur**ed. "But they said our fire was too dangerous and they wouldn't let us in."

Ember remembered how **furious** Bernie had been. *"Tsh'à ts' shâ sh pfùkh, tkhò ts'? Khû kò shá sh!"* he had **holler**ed. "**How dare you** keep us out? **Shame on you!**"

"Go back to Fire Land!" the guard had shot back.

Everyone in line had laughed. "My dad was so angry,

and **embarrassed**," Ember said. "The building **flood**ed a few years later, so I missed my one chance to see a Vivisteria."

When she turned toward Wade, she was surprised to see tears in his eyes.

"You must have been *so* **scared**," he said.

"I was," Ember said softly. Then she **shook off** the **uncomfortable** memory. "How do you do that?" she asked.

"Do what?" Wade asked.

"**Draw** people in!" said Ember. "You got a whole **stadium** to connect with you. I can't even connect with *one* customer. My stupid temper always kicks in." She **droop**ed over the side of the basket.

"I guess I just say what I feel," said Wade. "And I don't think a temper is so bad. Sometimes when I **lose** *my* **temper**, I think it's just *me* trying to tell me something I'm not ready to hear."

Ember lifted her head. "That's **ridiculous**."

"Maybe . . . ," admitted Wade. Then he pointed at something below. "Hey, there! Put us down there!"

Ember steered the balloon toward a **culvert**. They **land**ed and climbed out beside two giant wooden doors that were slightly **ajar**.

"That's not right," said Wade, studying the doors. He **dip**ped his finger in the water **nearby** and tasted it. Then he started to **gag**. "Motor oil," he **confirm**ed. "Yup, this is the **source**!"

He led Ember through the doors to **investigate** and headed toward the main canal.

"Why's there no water?" asked Ember.

"Because the doors are broken," Wade explained. "This is supposed to catch **spillover** from those main canals, and—"

Just then, a giant cruise ship[4] rolled by. Its **wake trigger**ed a small tsunami[5] over the canal walls.

Wade **panic**ked. "Run for your life![6]" he cried.

They raced toward the culvert doors. Ember jumped through to **safety**, but Wade was caught on the other side, **cling**ing **desperately** to the door. "Ahhh!" he cried. "Help! Ahhh!"

---

4 **cruise ship** 유람선. 휴식과 항해를 즐길 수 있는 관광 목적으로 사용되는 여객선. 선박 내에 음식점, 수영장, 오락 시설 등 각종 부대시설을 갖추고 있는 것이 특징이다.

5 **tsunami** 쓰나미. 바다 밑에서 일어나는 지진이나 화산 폭발 등으로 인해 갑자기 해안에 거대한 파도가 밀려오는 현상.

6 **run for your life** '살고 싶으면 뛰어' 라는 의미로, 매우 위험한 상황에서 필사적으로 대피해야 할 때 쓰는 표현.

Ember blazed into action. She melted a piece of rebar[7] off the door and **thrust** it toward Wade. "Grab this!" she cried.

He **grasp**ed it and she **tug**ged him through the door to safety. Then Ember saw the **steam**ing tops of Firetown buildings in the distance—exactly where the rushing water was heading. "Firetown!" she said with a gasp.

She raced out of the culvert toward a **pile** of sandbags and picked one up. "Catch!" she called.

Wade turned just as the sandbag hit him. *Bam!* It **splatter**ed him to the ground, but he rolled back up to his feet. He **struggle**d against the flow of water to carry the sandbag toward the broken doors.

Water still poured through the doors. With **grit**ted teeth, Wade carried the sandbag with one arm and used his free arm to press against the flow of water. His body **undulate**d against the **pressure**, but he was able to push the water back.

Finally, Wade **heave**d the sandbag toward the base of the doors. Then he called up. "Ember! Throw me more!"

They piled on sandbags, one by one. Ember threw them

---

7 **rebar** 철근. 철로 만든 막대기 모양의 건축 자재. 주로 콘크리트 속에 넣어 콘크리트를 더 튼튼하게 보강하고, 건물의 뼈대를 세우는 데 쓰인다.

down and Wade **stack**ed them up. When the bags were piled high, the water *finally* stopped. They set the last sandbag **in place**—together.

As Ember **caught her breath**, she studied the bags. "So, will this hold?"

Wade pushed against the bags, testing them. "Yup, it should for sure. At least long enough for me to get a city **crew** to fix it before Friday."

Ember didn't **catch** every word. She was too **distracted** by a **clump** of sand stuck to Wade's face.

He caught her staring. "What?"

"You've got a little . . . sand," Ember said, pointing.

"Oh." Wade **poke**d **around** in his face, trying to find it. "Here? Here?"

Ember reached out, nearly touching his **cheek**. "It's right there," she said. "Um . . ." She **yank**ed her hand back before she made him boil.

"Oh." Wade **pluck**ed out the clump of sand. "Thanks."

They fell silent for a moment, their eyes **lock**ed.

"Well . . . let me know when it's done, I guess," said Ember.

"I'll make sure there's a city crew here by Friday," said Wade.

"Okay," she added. "See ya." She turned and started to walk away.

"Wait!" Wade **blurt**ed. He **lower**ed his eyes, suddenly nervous, and asked, "Any chance you're free tomorrow? To **hang out** with a Water guy?"

"With a Water guy?" Ember smiled. "My dad would boil you alive."

"He doesn't have to know!" Wade **insist**ed. "We could meet in the city. I promise nothing weird. . . . Maybe a little pruning?" he joked, shrugging his shoulders.

Ember laughed, but then she caught herself and stopped. "Sorry," she said, turning away. "That's not going to happen."

"You smiled!" Wade called after her. "I saw it! Tomorrow? I'll be at Alkali[8] Theater. Three o'clock!" He **grin**ned.

Ember kept walking. Wade couldn't see it, but she was smiling, too.

---

8 **alkali** 알칼리. 강한 염기성을 띠는 물질로 산을 중화시키는 역할을 한다. 엘리멘트 시티는 원소들의 도시인 만큼 화학과 관련된 표현과 설정이 자주 등장하는데, 여기에서는 '알칼리'가 극장 이름으로 쓰였다.

Chapter 10

At Bernie's shop the next afternoon, Flarry and Flarrietta sat at their regular table playing chess.[1] **Bucket**s hung overhead to catch **drip**ping water. A **trickle** of water dripped onto the chessboard, **snuff**ing out a **fiery** piece.

"Oh!" cried Flarry. "Your **ceiling** is dripping again."

"More **leak**s?" Bernie **grumble**d, **glancing** up.

"Don't worry," said Ember. She **hop**ped onto a table and melted the **leaky** pipe shut with her hands. "This whole problem is going away. I can feel it."

---

1 **chess** 체스. 장기와 유사한 서양의 놀이. 두 사람이 8X8의 놀이 판에서 각기 16개의 말을 정해진 규칙에 따라 움직여 상대편의 왕(King)을 움직이지 못하게 하면 이기는 게임.

Ember hopped down. Then she checked the time. It was almost three o'clock—time to meet Wade!

"And since we're all good, I'm also going away . . . to do **deliveries!**"

As Ember rushed past her mother, Cinder **sniff**ed the air. Her face **lit up.** "Do I smell something on . . . *Ember?*" she **exclaim**ed, laughing with **glee.**

Her daughter was finally in *love.* Cinder was certain of it.

As Ember hurried out the front door, Clod suddenly appeared. "Yo, Ember!"

"Ah, Clod!" she said, **startled.**

"I grew another one!" he **announce**d. He **pop**ped a **tiny** flower out of his **armpit,** then offered it to Ember. "My queen."

Ember touched the flower and again . . . *Poof!* It burned up. "Oops, sorry," she said. "But gotta go." She left Clod behind and hurried toward the movie theater across town.

Wade was waiting for her beneath a **marquee** that read TIDE AND PREJUDICE.[2] When he saw Ember coming, he

---

2 **Tide and Prejudice** 영국의 소설가 제인 오스틴(Jane Austen)이 지은 장편 소설 '오만과 편견 (Pride and Prejudice)'에서 'Pride' 대신 물의 원소와 관련된 비슷한 발음의 'Tide(조류)'를 넣어 재치 있게 바꾼 표현.

teared up. She had actually come! He tried to **pull himself together** as they **head**ed into the theater.

When the lights **dim**med inside, Ember's **flame**s shone bright. *Too* bright. All around her, **audience** members **scowl**ed. She pulled her hood tightly around her flames and **slunk** into her seat.

After the movie, Wade and Ember **wander**ed along the street, stopping at a photo **booth**. Wade made **goofy** faces, but Ember's **glow** blew out the exposure.[3] The only thing **visible** in the photos were two sets of white **eyeball**s.

Later, they **board**ed an elevator to an **observation** deck that looked out over the city. As more people **crowd**ed into the elevator, Ember and Wade **squeeze**d together so close, they were nearly touching.

When they arrived on the deck, a few kids **shrank** from Ember's flames. But she knew how to **put them at ease**. She blew smoke rings that **transform**ed into **silly** faces.

As the kids **cheer**ed, Ember took a **bow**. Wade gazed at her with watery, **adoring** eyes. The kids seemed to like Ember

---

3 **exposure** 노출. 사진을 촬영할 때 렌즈로 들어오는 빛의 양을 조절하는 기기 조작 과정으로, 노출 값이 높을 수록 사진이 밝아진다.

almost as much as he did.

Almost.

The next day at Bernie's shop, Ember sat at the **counter** with a notebook. Inside, she **doodle**d ideas for a new sign. She also **snuck** glances at the photo **strip** of her and Wade **tuck**ed beneath the notebook.

When a customer lit a **sparkler** before buying it, Ember grabbed it from him. Her flames **churn**ed, but she **took a breath** to **compose** herself. She calmly handed the sparkler back to the customer.

As Ember **stole** another glance at Wade's photo, Bernie walked up, startling her. Had he seen the picture? Ember covered it up with her notebook and a nervous smile. When Bernie walked away, she **sigh**ed with **relief**.

But Cinder had seen everything. When Ember left the counter, Cinder snuck over and lifted the notebook. She studied the photo strip.

"Who *is* this guy?" Cinder wondered **aloud**.

She was **determined** to find out.

Ember and Wade **hung out** again, this time at an **outdoor** café. A waiter **breeze**d past, dropping off **mug**s of a pink drink. Wade **down**ed his in one **gulp**—and **immediately** turned purple.

Ember tried to drink hers, but the liquid boiled away before it even touched her lips.

Suddenly, people around them started dancing. It was a flash mob![4] Wade hopped up and **bounce**d his **sloshy stomach** to the music. He waved for Ember to join him.

Wade **stretch**ed like a **stream** around Ember's **flickering** moves. Then people started coupling off and dancing together. When Wade held out his hand to Ember, she **froze**. She wanted to take it, but how could she? Her heat would boil him! She was **relieved** when a couple danced by too closely, knocking Wade backward into a **fountain**.

He **emerge**d seconds later, **spout**ing water from his mouth and posing like a fountain **statue**. Ember couldn't help

---

4 **flash mob** 플래시 몹. 불특정 다수의 사람들이 정해진 시간과 장소에 모여 주어진 행동을 하고 곧바로 흩어지는 행위.

grinning a little.

The next time Ember and Wade met up, they **stroll**ed around Mineral[5] Lake, where colorful crystals[6] grew along the **shore**. When Ember stepped on a crystal, her orange flame turned green.

"Whoa," said Wade. "How'd you do that?"

She picked up the loose crystal. "It's the minerals," she said. "Check this out." Ember **race**d along the lake, her fire changing colors based on which mineral she stepped on.

Wade laughed **out loud**. "**Awesome!**"

As Ember **leap**ed onto a high **cluster** of crystals, he blew out his breath. "Wow." Then he had an idea. "Watch this!"

Wade raced onto the **surface** of the lake and **skid**ded across, spraying a fine **mist** in the air. The mist caught the sun's **rays** and **reflect**ed a rainbow of color.

When Wade came to a stop, Ember—all **aglow**—gazed at

---

5   **mineral** 미네랄 혹은 광물(鑛物). 자연에 주로 고체 상태로 존재하며, 각 부분의 질이 균일하고 화학 성분이 일정한 물질. 석탄, 철, 금, 은 등 약 3,800개 이상의 종류가 알려져 있다.

6   **crystal** 크리스털. '수정'이라고도 부르며, 투명하고 형태가 뚜렷한 광물을 가리킨다. 불순물의 혼합 정도에 따라 다양한 빛을 띤다.

him. He was **definitely** starting to **grow on** her.

Later, when Ember walked home alone under the **elevated** Wetro, it **whiz**zed overhead, sending a wall of water down from the track. But this time, Ember didn't pop an umbrella.

She **long**ed to touch the water. She reached out her hand but **hesitate**d a moment too long. The water **vanish**ed as the train **disappear**ed along the tracks.

Bernie's shop lay just beyond the tracks. Ember pulled her flames together[7] and hurried through the door into the familiar shop.

But the next day, in the culvert **uptown**, water began leaking through the sandbags she and Wade had so carefully stacked. And that water began to slowly flow toward Firetown.

---

7 **pull her flames together** '정신을 가다듬다'라는 뜻의 숙어인 'pull oneself together'에 'flame(불꽃)'이라는 단어를 넣어, 불의 종족인 엠버가 자신의 정신을 가다듬었다는 의미로 쓰였다.

Chapter 11

The next morning, a **shallow** river of water raced through the **canal** near Bernie's shop. Inside, Bernie struggled to make kol nuts while Ember climbed to a high **shelf** to get something for a customer.

"Sòbê sh sfá," said the customer. "I'll take that one."

"Another?" asked Ember.

"Ìshkshá," replied the customer. "Please."

Ember reached for a bottle on the top shelf just as the walls of the shop **rumbled** and shook. A **chunk** of drywall[1]

---

1   **drywall** 석고 보드. 두꺼운 판지 사이에 석고 반죽을 넣어 굳힌 재료로, 벽이나 천장 등을 시공하는 데 쓰이는 건축 재료.

fell off the wall and **crash**ed to the floor near the Blue Flame. Water **gush**ed from a pipe in the wall shooting out toward the Blue Flame.

Bernie **hop**ped to his feet, **desperate** to save the Flame.

"No!" cried Ember.

"The water is back!" Bernie hollered.

Together, they struggled to move the Blue Flame. Bernie began to **cough**.

As Ember melted the **leaky** pipe, someone called from the door. "Ember Lumen? **Delivery** for Ember Lumen?"

A delivery person entered carrying several vases of flowers. From across the room, Ember could see two eyes in the water inside one of the vases.

Cinder reached the delivery person first. "Flowers for Ember?" she said in a **giddy** voice.

Ember **gasp**ed. She finished fixing the pipe and hurried to collect the flowers. "Oh, excuse me. Hee-hee, these are beautiful," she said. "I'm going to put these away." She **dart**ed toward the **basement**.

As Ember set the vases on the basement floor, she **whisper**ed, "What are you doing here?"

Wade popped his head out of a vase. "I got bad news," he said as he began **pour**ing water from the other vases onto his head. With each pour, he grew taller and his body **fill**ed **out**. "The sandbags didn't hold."

"Uh, **obviously**!" said Ember.

"Yeah. And I also got worse news." He pulled some flowers from his head and **toss**ed them to the floor. "I'd forgotten a *tiny* **detail** about the last time I saw that city **crew**."

Wade explained how his ex-**boss** had **remind**ed him of something. "You **knock**ed over three tons of cement[2] dust," his ex-boss had said. "Half the guys still haven't **recover**ed!"

Wade could still **picture** the angry **construction** workers— Water guys who had frozen like **statue**s as the cement dust **coat**ing their bodies **eventually harden**ed.

"I guess you could say they still have *hard* feelings," he said, **chuckling** at his own joke. "Because they won't help us."

"Wade," said Ember, "Gale's **deadline** is tomorrow. We need more sandbags!"

"But that didn't work before," Wade reminded her.

---

2 cement 시멘트. 석고와 진흙 등 각종 물질을 섞어서 만든 건축용 접착제.

"Well, I can't just do *nothing!*" Ember fired back, **exasperated**.

Suddenly, the basement door **burst** open. "Ember, did you fix the leak?" her father called as he started down the stairs. Bernie gasped when he saw Wade. "It's you again!"

Wade glanced over his shoulder, as if Bernie were talking to someone else. "Who, me?" Wade asked, **confused**.

"You're the guy who started all this!" shouted Bernie. He grabbed a fireplace poker and **swung** it at Wade.

"Ahhh!" **yell**ed Wade.

"No, Dad!" said Ember. "Different guy. Not all Water looks alike."

But Bernie looked at Wade's **badge**. "You are a city **inspector**?"

Wade glanced down, **busted**. "Uhh . . ."

"No!" Ember answered for Wade. "Right?" She **shot** Wade a look, willing him to **play along**.

"Right," Wade **confirm**ed **uncertainly**. "I am not an inspector." He put his hand over his badge, but his water only **magnified** it. The word *inspector* grew larger.

Wade tried again, covering the badge with his other arm.

But the word grew even larger.

Bernie stared at it. "You *are* an inspector," he said. "Why are you **poking around**? Is this because of the water leak?"

"No!" said Ember. "Not because of water in *any* way. He's a different kind of inspector. Right?" She glanced again at Wade.

"Yeah, yeah, I'm a . . ." He **fumble**d to find the words. "I'm a . . . *food* inspector. I've come to **inspect** your food." He stood tall, trying to look **official**.

"Hmm," Bernie said to Ember. "I think he's lying through his feet."

"Teeth," corrected Ember.

"Whatever!" Bernie said. Then he turned back toward Wade. "The food is upstairs. Come."

As Bernie led the way upstairs to the shop, Ember shot Wade a look. "Food inspector?" she **hiss**ed.

"I panicked!" he whispered.

Ember **grunt**ed with **frustration**.

In the shop, Bernie **slam**med a bowl of burning kol nuts on the counter in front of Wade. Wade gulped and laughed **nervously**.

"Are you really a food inspector?" **interrogate**d Bernie.

"As far as you know, yeah," Wade said.

"Then inspect *this*," said Bernie, **gesturing** toward the burning kol nuts.

Ember stepped forward. "Dad . . . ," she began.

Bernie **silence**d her. He pushed the bowl closer to Wade.

Wade leaned over and sniffed. His **nostril**s bubbled from the heat. "Yep, looks all good to me," he confirmed.

"No," said Bernie. "Inspect it with your mouth." He **demonstrate**d by eating a kol nut and blowing fire.

Wade smiled weakly. He **scoop**ed up a kol nut with a spoon. He blew on the nut as if that would make any difference. Then, as the customers in the shop **held their breath**, he took a **scalding bite**.

Everyone watched as the kol nut **sizzle**d down Wade's clear, watery throat. Then the pain hit him, and his smile disappeared. Wade **let out** a scream before **clamp**ing his hands over his mouth.

Bernie watched with a **satisfied smirk** as a **massive** air bubble rose through Wade's face.

Pop! It burst a hole in the top of his head, releasing hissing

steam.

"You see?" Ember said quickly. "He likes it!"

Wade started coughing, but then he stopped himself, holding it in. He smiled and gave a thumbs-up. When he tried to speak, he could only **nod**. His throat was burning.

Bernie laughed and reached for another bucket of kol nuts. These were even hotter than the others. "You must try these. They're straight from Fire Land." He poured some of the kol nuts into Wade's dish.

"Dad, those are too hot," Ember **caution**ed.

"I'm okay," **croak**ed Wade. "I love hot food."

He took another bite, and his head filled with air bubbles. *Pop! Pop! Pop!* Water burst from the holes, forcing Wade backward. He sprayed water all over the shop.

"Hey, watch your water!" cried Bernie. "So, did we pass?"

"Mm-hmm," said Wade. "A-plus.[3]" He **straighten**ed up. "Actually, after the heat **dies down**, that's really good." He pointed at the kol nuts. "If you don't mind . . ."

Wade grabbed a cup and scooped up another **portion** of

---

3 **A-plus** 알파벳으로 표기하는 평가 체계에서 받을 수 있는 최고 점수 혹은 등급.

kol nuts. He dripped water onto them from his finger, and the nuts **smolder**ed and hissed.

Ember gasped. She **clear**ed **her throat**, trying to get Wade's **attention**. This was going to burn her father up! She **slid** her hand across her neck as if to say, *Cut! Stop! Please!*

But Wade didn't take the hint. He took a drink from the **mug** and **smack**ed **his lips**. "See, it's really tasty if you **water** it **down** a little. . . ."

"Water us down!" Bernie **explode**d. "Water us down! Where's the camera?" He pulled an **instant** camera from behind the counter and **snap**ped a photo of Wade's **terrified** face.

"We will *never* be watered down by you," **declare**d Bernie. "Get out!"

Ember hurried toward Wade. "All right, sir," she said. "You gotta go."

As Wade backed out of the shop, Bernie was still **huff**ing and **glaring**.

"Dad, don't worry," Ember called to him. "I got this." She followed Wade out the door.

Bernie **let loose** a string of Firish as they left.

"Look, meet me at the beach and we'll make more sandbags," said Ember outside the shop. "We have to **figure out** how to fix those doors."

They **lock**ed eyes for a moment, and then Wade hurried away.

Back inside the shop, Bernie was still **seething**. "Water wants to water us down?" he said. "Then water is no longer allowed in the shop!"

He **pin**ned Wade's photo to the wall under a **Ban**ned sign. "He is panned!" Bernie declared.

"Um . . . banned," Ember **gently** corrected.

"Banned!" **echo**ed Bernie. He was so **agitated**, he started coughing **intensely**.

Ember had never seen her father cough so hard. She **rush**ed to **comfort** him. "*Àshfá,* it's okay," she **soothe**d. "It's all going to be okay."

But as she glanced up at Wade's photo on the wall, she wasn't so sure.

Chapter 12

That night on the beach, as the sun was setting, Ember **shovel**ed sand into a bag. It was **exhausting** work, but she was **determined**.

Wade held the bag open. "I don't think this is going to work," he **confess**ed.

"Well, it won't unless you hold the bag straight," Ember argued.

Wade **adjust**ed the bag. "Maybe your dad will understand," he said gently.

Ember **scoff**ed and continued shoveling.

"I'm serious," said Wade. "Look, I know it can be **tough**.

I mean with my dad . . . we were like oil and water. I never got a chance to fix that." His voice was heavy with **regret**. "But you guys are different. It might be time to tell him."

Ember shoveled faster. "Yeah, right," she said. "And tell him what? That I got us **shut down** and destroyed his dream?"

Ember let out a **furious** yell. Then she **collapse**d to her knees. Her fire **simmer**ed to a soft, gentle candlelight. As she calmed down, her **prismatic inner** light showed through.

"I think I'm failing," she **murmur**ed. "My *àshfá* should have **retire**d *years* ago, but he doesn't think I'm ready. You have no idea how hard they've worked or what they've had to **endure**. The family they left behind . . ." She **pause**d and then finally asked the question that was burning in her heart. "How do you **repay** a **sacrifice** that big? It all feels like a **burden**. How can I say that?"

Ember **sank** lower and hung her head. "I'm a bad daughter," she whispered.

Wade **crouch**ed beside her. "Hey, no," he said. "You're doing your best."

Ember sniffed. "I'm a **mess**," she said with a small laugh. She fired up her flames, trying to cover her **vulnerable** light.

"Nah," said Wade. "I think you're even more beautiful."

When he **grin**ned, Ember smiled back. "Maybe you're right when you said my temper is trying to tell me something," she **admit**ted.

That was when Wade noticed the sand beneath Ember. "Whoa, look what your fire did to the sand," he said. "It's glass!"

Ember picked up a piece of glass and **melt**ed it in her hands. She formed it into a **sphere** and created a design inside, something that **reflect**ed how she was feeling.

Wade watched her, **mesmerize**d. He had never seen anyone do something like that before. "It looks like a Vivisteria flower," he said.

Suddenly, Ember had an idea. "I know how to **seal** those doors!" she announced. She hopped up and started to run, leaving the glass Vivisteria in the sand.

Wade followed close behind, wondering what this amazing Fire girl had in mind and how he could help her.

When darkness fell, Ember and Wade were working at the **culvert**. Ember stood before the **stack** of sandbags holding the doors shut. She **inhale**d deeply and pressed her hands against the bags, and then there was an **explosion** of light.

But this time she controlled her **blast**, as if she were painting with fire. Ember glowed with joy.

Wade **admire**d her **radiant** light as she worked. She seemed so . . . free.

When Ember finished, she stood back and **caught her breath**. She had melted the sand into a thick wall of glass! She sighed with **satisfaction**. But Wade **bit** his lip. He **sniffle**d, and then he let the tears flow.

"Are you crying?" Ember gently **tease**d.

"Yes!" he **sob**bed. "I've just never been **punch**ed in the face with beauty before."

Suddenly, the **earth** began to **vibrate**. Ember gasped as an **enormous** boat passed through the canal, sending **sheet**s of water into the culvert.

Ember and Wade **stare**d at the glass wall as the water rushed in behind it. They took a couple of steps backward, ready to run. But the glass held. Water **splash**ed only into the bottom of the culvert behind the doors.

"It worked!" cried Ember.

"I'll have Gale come by right after work," Wade promised. "I'll let you know the second I hear anything."

"You think this'll be good enough for her?" Ember asked.

"Honestly?" said Wade. "It's hard to know. She could go either way."

Ember nodded nervously. Then Wade took something out of his pocket very carefully. "Oh, here . . . I saved this for you," he said, handing her the glass Vivisteria. "It's special."

Ember silently accepted her **creation**. Had she really made something so beautiful?

The next night, Ember sat in her room, admiring the glass Vivisteria. She turned it over and over in her hands. Then she heard her father coughing.

Ember hurried downstairs and found Bernie **repair**ing a wall. When he coughed again, she asked, "Àshfá, you okay?"

Bernie smiled. "Yes, yes. There's just too much to fix."

Ember pulled a metal stool[1] toward him and took a seat.

---

1 stool 스툴. 등받이와 팔걸이가 없는 둥근 형태의 작은 의자.

"I'll take care of it," she said. "*You* need to rest. And that's an order." She gave him her most **stern expression**.

"Yes, ma'am!" Bernie **salute**d.

They both laughed, and then Bernie took her hands. "Ember, I see a change in you," he said. "Happier. Calmer with customers, and with that . . . *food inspector*." He **spat** the last two words as he glanced at Wade's photo on the wall.

"You're always putting the shop first," Bernie continued. "You have **prove**d I can trust you." Then he began to cough again. His hand **flicker**ed, but he quickly hid it from Ember. "I'm so lucky I have you," he said before starting up the stairs.

Ember's smile **faded**. She stared at the picture of Wade on the "**ban**ned" board. Had he heard back from Gale yet? She had to find out. She had to see Wade right now.

Chapter 13

Cinder, who had been sleeping, suddenly sat upright and **sniff**ed the air.

Cinder sniffed again. "Love!" she **declare**d.

Downstairs, Ember **lock**ed the shop door and **snuck** toward her scooter. She quietly pushed it away from the shop, then started the engine and drove off.

Cinder followed her out the front door. She **suspiciously** sniffed the air and **head**ed after Ember, following her **scent**.

Ember drove to Water Town, where **canal**s flowed freely and ice-blue[1] buildings **stream**ed **skyward**. When she reached

---

1   **ice-blue** 아이스 블루. 얼음에서 보이는 청색과 같이 파스텔 톤의 연한 파란색.

Wade's mom's apartment, she **glance**d up at the **grand entrance**, which was **surround**ed by **cascading waterfall**s. Ember **gulp**ed.

A large Water guy with a **mustache guard**ed the front door. Ember hurried toward the door just as Wade opened it. "Ember!" he said. "You found it! Everything okay?"

"Please tell me that you have some good news from Gale," she said. "I'm getting really worried about my dad. This has to break my way."

"Yeah, I haven't heard from her yet," said Wade, "but she *swore* she'd call tonight. Actually, my family stopped by for dinner. You want to come up and wait for the call together?"

Ember **hesitate**d. "Your family?" she said.

Just around the corner, out of view, a member of Ember's own family was **hot on Ember's trail**. Cinder sniffed the air and caught Ember's scent. When she saw Ember talking in the doorway of the large building, Cinder **duck**ed. Who was Ember talking to? Cinder **peer**ed over a **ledge** but couldn't quite see.

"Okay, I'll come up for a bit," Cinder heard Ember say.

As Ember **gaze**d up again at the **ritzy** building, she caught her breath. "I'm sorry, you *live* here?" she asked Wade.

He **shrug**ged. "It's my mom's place."

"Oh my gosh," said Ember. She followed him into the building, past the Water doorman.

Cinder hurried up to the doorman and tried to walk in, too. "I'm afraid I can't let you in," he said. "**Resident**s and guests only."

She pretended to leave, then **spun** sideways and tried to **dodge** the doorman. But he **extend**ed his arm, creating a wall of water.

Cinder spun the other way and he **block**ed her again.

"Ah, okay. I *understand*," she said. "You're surprisingly good at your job!"

"You're surprisingly fast for your age," he responded.

"You have *no* idea," Cinder warned. As she spun her **flame**s into a small tornado,[2] the doorman's eyes **widen**ed.

Upstairs, Wade's mom, Brook, warmly **greet**ed Ember. "Ember! I'm so excited to finally meet you," said Brook. The

---

2 **tornado** 토네이도. 바다나 넓은 평지에서 발생하는 매우 강력한 회오리바람으로, 깔때기 같은 모양을 특징으로 한다.

tall, **elegant** Water woman **lean**ed forward. "Do we hug, or . . . wave, or . . . don't want to **put** you **out**. Ha, ha!"

"Um," Ember smiled nervously, "a hello is fine."

"Hardly," Brook argued. "Wade hasn't stopped talking about you since the day you met. The boy is **smitten!**"

"Mom!" cried Wade, **mortified**.

"Oh, come on," said Brook. "I'm your mother. I know when something's **light**ing you **up**. I just didn't know she would be so *smoky!*" Brook **fake**d a cough at Ember's "smokiness," and they all laughed.

Ember stopped laughing first.

"Come this way," said Brook, waving them inside. "Meet the rest of the family."

Ember followed, until she saw that the apartment was one big swimming pool filled with **float**ing **furniture**. It was not designed for Fire **Element**s. In fact, it felt a little dangerous.

Wade reached for a golden **floaty** chair and held it so that Ember could climb in. But it was too **flammable**. So Wade covered it with the less-flammable welcome mat from the **foyer**.

Ember finally **made it** into the chair, but she **wobble**d **precariously**.

As Wade guided Ember into the pool, Brook **exclaim**ed, "Oh, honey! You won't believe what your baby niece did today! She . . . she smiled." Brook **immediately** teared up, which got Wade going, too.

"No, she didn't," he **blubber**ed.

Brook nodded, and then they both burst into tears.

Ember stared, wide-eyed. Wade's family was so different from her own.

When they followed Brook through a waterfall curtain, Wade held his arm above Ember to keep her dry. They **emerge**d into a dining room full of Water Elements sitting at an **inflatable** dining table.

"Hey, everyone!" said Wade. "This is Ember!"

"Hey!" said a Water guy who looked a lot like Wade. He wore a chef's **apron** and a **cheery** smile.

"That's my brother Alan," said Wade, "and his wife, Eddy."

Eddy, a curly-haired woman in a sweater, waved at Ember. "Hi!"

"And we got two kids that are swimming around here

somewhere," said Alan. "Marco![3]"

A young Water boy **pop**ped out of the water.

"Polo!" Alan called again.

Another kid emerged. "Hi, Uncle Wade!" Polo **holler**ed.

When the kids saw Ember, they stared. "Do you die if you fall in water?" Marco asked. He **jostle**d her floaty chair.

"Whoa!" said Ember.

"Marco!" Wade **scold**ed.

Alan **flush**ed with **embarrassment**. "Kids, hee-hee," he said to Ember. "Don't hate us."

As the kids swam away, Ember **regain**ed her balance— and tried to smile.

"Anyway," said Wade, pulling her floaty toward the dinner table, "that's my little **sib**, Lake. And their girlfriend, Ghibli."

" 'Sup,[4]" said Ghibli, peering at Ember from beneath a swoop of hair.[5]

"They're students at Element City School for the Arts,"

---

3 **Marco** 영미권 아이들이 수영장에서 하는 술래잡기 놀이의 일종인 '마르코 폴로(Marco Polo)' 놀이에서 따온 이름. 이 놀이에서 술래가 '마르코(Marco)'하고 외치면, 주변 아이들은 '폴로(Polo)'하고 대답을 해야 하며 술래는 그 소리만을 듣고 사람들을 찾아야 한다.

4 **'sup** '안녕', '잘 지내?'라는 뜻의 인사말 'What's up?'의 구어적인 표현.

5 **a swoop of hair** '급강하, 위에서 덮치기'라는 뜻의 영단어 'swoop'에서 유추할 수 있듯이, 앞머리를 전부 한쪽 방향으로 쓸어 내려 이마 전체 또는 눈을 가리는 머리 모양.

Wade explained.

"**Follow**ing **in Mom's wake**," added Lake.

"Oh, **nonsense**," said Brook, waving her hand. "I'm just an **architect**. The real artist is my brother Harold."

Harold, a short, broad Water man, held Polo under his arm. "Oh, I just **dabble** in watercolors,[6]" he said. "Or, as we like to call them, 'colors.'"

Brook placed a dish on the table and sat down. "Oh, don't listen to him," she said. "He's a wonderful painter. One of his paintings just got in the Element City Museum's **permanent collection**."

"Wow," said Ember. "That is so cool. My only **talent** is 'Cleanup on **aisle** four!'"

Wade **scoff**ed. "Talk about being **modest**. Ember's got an **incredible creative** flame! I've never seen anything like it." He **cast** her a loving glance.

Harold looked at Ember, too. "I just have to say," he said, a bit too loudly and slowly, "that you speak *so* well and clear—"

Wade shot his uncle a look, but Ember **kept her cool**.

---

6 **watercolor** 수채화 물감. 물에 풀어서 쓰는 물감으로, 물을 이용해 물감의 농도를 조절하여 색의 미묘한 변화와 투명도를 표현할 수 있다.

"Yeah, it's amazing what talking in the same language your entire life can do," she said.

"Doh!" said Harold, **embarrassed** at his **inappropriate comment**.

Alan quickly changed the **subject** to break the **tension**. "Hey, Ember, did Wade ever tell you that he's **deathly** afraid of sponges?"

"No," said Ember, **intrigued**.

"I was **traumatized**," said Wade.

He explained how as a **kindergartner**, he had been walking with his class when a **janitor** dropped a huge sponge. Curious, Wade touched it with his finger—and the sponge began **suck**ing in his water. He had tried to pull away, **panic**king, but the **suction** was too strong. It **soak**ed him up **entirely**!

When Wade finished the story, everyone laughed except him. Even Ember **let out** a **chuckle**—she couldn't help it!

"I still can't use a sponge around him!" said Brook.

"I was **stuck** in there for hours," said Wade **defensively**.

Alan reached for a pitcher, but he was laughing so hard, the **pitcher slip**ped from his hand and **shatter**ed.

"Alan! That was new!" his mother scolded.

"My bad," Alan **apologize**d. "I'm all whirlpools[7] tonight."

Ember picked up two large **shard**s of glass and blew on them, melting them back together. "I can fix it," she **reassure**d Alan. She **gather**ed the rest of the broken pieces and melted them into a glowing liquid **orb**. Then she blew it into a shape **resembling** a pitcher.

As Ember worked, her **inner** light cast rainbows across the room. She was so lost in her creative process, she **barely** noticed that everyone was watching her.

With one last **twist** and pull, Ember formed the handle of the pitcher. She **tweak**ed the **spout** and set the pitcher back on the table. Then she saw the others staring.

Ember zipped up her fire. "Oh, um, sorry," she said quickly.

"That was incredible," **gush**ed Harold.

The whole family began **cheer**ing and **applaud**ing.

Ember's face burned. "It's just melted glass," she said **modestly**.

"Just melted glass?" **echo**ed Brook. "Every building in the

---

7 **whirlpool** 원래 '소용돌이'라는 뜻이지만, 여기에서는 물의 원소가 소란을 일으키는 상황을 나타내는 표현으로 쓰였다.

new city is built from 'just melted glass.' "

Ember glanced out the windows for the first time and **admire**d the view of the Water **District**. Brook **had a point**.

"Oh no," added Brook, "you have to do something with that talent."

Wade leaned toward Ember. "See?" he whispered. "I told you you're special."

Ember smiled back, suddenly believing him.

Then Wade got an idea. "Ooh, thought bubble!" he **announce**d. "Maybe after dinner we play the Crying Game?"

Excited murmurs circled the table.

"Let me guess," said Ember. "You try to cry?"

"We try *not* to cry," Wade corrected her.

After dinner, it was game time. Brook and Harold **face**d **off** against each other first. Wade **flip**ped over an **hourglass** timer and said, "You have one minute. Go!"

Harold spoke first. "Nineteen seventy-nine. November. You—"

Brook **instantly** burst into tears. Her team—Wade, Lake, and Eddy—threw up their hands while the other team—Alan and Ghibli—**celebrate**d.

"—never got a chance to say goodbye to Nana," **bawl**ed Brook before Harold could say another word.

"Okay, Ember, Wade," said Harold. "You're up."

Ember and Wade faced off.

"Yeah, this is almost **unfair**," Ember **point**ed **out**, "because I have **literally** never cried. You've got no chance."

"Sounds like a **challenge**," said Wade with a grin.

Harold flipped the timer. "Ready, go!" he declared.

"Butterfly. **Windshield** wipers.[8] Half a butterfly," Wade said simply.

His family **sniffle**d and sobbed, but Ember sat still as a **statue, unmoved**. So Wade tried again. "Okay, an old man on his **deathbed** remembers the summer he fell in love. She was out of his **league**, and he was young and **scared**." Wade sniffled, his own words getting to him. "He let her go, thinking surely summer would come again." He sniffled again. "It never did."

Wade did his best to **hold back** his own tears. But still, Ember's eyes were dry.

---

8 **wiper** 와이퍼. 자동차의 앞유리에 흘러내리는 빗방울이나 눈을 좌우로 움직이면서 닦아 내는 장치.

"Almost out of time," Harold blubbered.

Wade **realize**d he was going to need a different **approach**. He tried again. "Ember, when I met you, I thought I was **drown**ing. But that light, that light inside you, has made me feel so alive. And all I want now is to be near it—near you. Together."

He stared into Ember's eyes, which reflected his own image back at him. He looked deeper, so deep that he could almost see her there beside him, **shed**ding her outer light.

As he gazed at her, he saw something **startling**. A white-hot **lava** tear drop rolled down her **cheek** and **land**ed in the water with a *hiss*.

For a few seconds, no one moved. Wade, Ember, and Wade's entire family were caught up in the moment. Then . . .

Ring! Ring!

The phone broke the silence.

Wade hurried to pick it up. "Hello?" he said. "Gale, hi."

Chapter 14

Across town, Gale stood at the culvert with a few Air city workers. "Glass?" she said into the phone to Wade. "You **repair**ed it with glass?"

Gale watched as an Air worker tested the glass by **punch**ing it. *Poof!* His hand **disappear**ed. Another worker raised a **hammer**, about to hit the glass.

"Hold the storm[1] . . . ," said Gale, watching.

On the other end of the line, Wade **swallow**ed hard. Ember anxiously waited.

---

1   **hold the storm** '기다려'라는 뜻의 'hold it'에 'storm(폭풍)'이라는 단어를 넣어서, 공기 종족이 사용하는 말로 바꾸었다.

Gale saw that the glass held against the force of the hammer. "*Tempered* glass?[2]" she said. "**Solid** as a rock. I like it. Consider the **ticket**s cancelled."

As Wade **hung up**, he broke into a **teary**-eyed smile.

"We did it?" Ember **incredulously** asked.

"Yup!" said Wade.

Later, when it was time to go, Ember **approach**ed Wade's mother. "Thank you, Mrs. Ripple," she said. "This was . . . this was really great."

Brook held the repaired glass **pitcher** in her hands. "Yeah, it was," she agreed. "And I mean what I said about your **talent**. I have a friend who runs the best glassmaking firm in the world. During dinner, I **slip**ped out and I made a call. And I told her about you. They're looking for an intern.[3] It could be an amazing **opportunity**."

Ember **glow**ed with excitement. "For real?"

"It's a long way from the city, but it would be an **incredible** start," **gush**ed Brook. "You have a bright future." Then she

---

2 **tempered glass** 강화 유리. 고열로 처리하여 일반 유리보다 3~5배 단단하게 만든 유리로, 충격과 급격한 온도 변화에 잘 견딜 수 있다.

3 **intern** 인턴. 회사에 정식으로 채용되지 않은 채로 실습 과정을 밟는 사원.

glanced down at the pitcher in her hands. "Look at me! I have an original Ember!"

Ember smiled **nervously** as she turned to go. An internship at a glassmaking firm *would* be an amazing opportunity. But how could Ember ever leave her father and the shop? He needed her.

"Hold up," called Wade. "I'll **walk** you out."

Downstairs, Cinder was still **spar**ring with the doorman. By now, the doorman was a half-steamed waterwall. Cinder's **fiery** tornado had slowed to a stop, and she was trying to **catch her breath**.

"I'm afraid you're still going to have to wait out here, ma'am," the doorman **huff**ed **and puff**ed.

"And I'm afraid . . . ," said Cinder, **gasp**ing, "I will **throw up**." **Dizzy** from spinning, she **stagger**ed toward the **bush**es right when Wade and Ember left the building.

As Ember hurried toward her scooter, Wade **race**d after her. "Ember!" he called. "Ember, hold up. What's going on?"

"I can't believe she basically offered me a job," **groan**ed Ember.

"I know!" said Wade. "Could be cool!"

"Yeah, super cool, Wade," she said **sarcastically**. "I could move out and make glass in a **faraway** city. Do whatever I want." Her flames **roil**ed.

"I don't understand," said Wade.

"I'm going home," said Ember. She started up her scooter.

"Fine," said Wade, "then I'm going with you." He **hop**ped on back, careful to leave a little space between himself and Ember's flames.

"Ugh!" cried Ember. She **rev**ved the scooter, **zip**ping into the night while Wade hung on **for dear life**.

Cinder **regain**ed her balance just **in time** to see them drive off. "A Water guy!" she **exclaim**ed.

"Look, my mom was just trying to be helpful!" Wade **yell**ed over the scooter's engine. "She doesn't know how excited you are to run the shop!"

"Arrgh!" Ember **growl**ed. She revved the scooter again, **weaving** through **traffic** so fast that Wade's body began to **stretch** out.

"What is the matter?" Wade cried.

"Nothing!" she **insist**ed.

"Yeah? Because we're going like a thousand and—"

Wade's eyes widened and he **gesture**d wildly. "Bus!"

His body stretched out even more as Ember **swerve**d to avoid the bus.

By the time they reached Firetown, Ember was going so fast that the wind **ripple**d her flames. "You don't know me, Wade! Okay?" she declared. "So stop pretending like you do."

"What is this about?" he hollered.

"Nothing," she said. "Everything. I don't know. It's . . ."

As they approached Bernie's shop, she hit the brakes and **skid**ded to a stop. Wade's body **slosh**ed back into shape. Through the dark windows of the shop, the Blue Flame **flicker**ed.

"I don't think I actually *do* want to run the shop, okay?" Ember admitted. "*That's* what my temper has been trying to tell me . . . I'm **trap**ped."

As she climbed off the scooter, she stared at the Blue Flame. "You know what's crazy? Even when I was a *kid,* I would pray to the Blue Flame to be good enough to **fill my father's shoes** someday. Because this place is his dream. But I never once asked . . . what *I* wanted to do." She **sigh**ed. "I think that's because deep down, I knew it didn't matter. Because the only way to **repay** a **sacrifice** so big is by sacrificing your life, too."

Wade searched for what to say to make Ember feel better. But someone else spoke first.

"Ember!" Cinder **descend**ed the stairs of the **nearby** Wetro **platform**. "Don't move!"

"Oh," **mutter**ed Ember. "My mother." She **froze** as Cinder hurried toward them, stopping a couple of times to catch her breath.

"Mom, it's okay," Ember started. "He's just a friend."

"Si—" Cinder **took another breath**, holding up her finger. "**Silence!**" she ordered, so loud that Ember gasped.

"I could smell you from over there!" said Cinder. "You **stink**."

Ember's face **flame**d. "What are you talking about?"

"*You* know what I'm talking about," replied her mother.

Ember **sniff**ed herself, and then it **dawn**ed on her. "You're smelling love on me?" She glanced at Wade and wondered . . . *was* she in love?

"If your father finds out . . . ," Cinder warned. "Fire and water cannot be together! I'll prove it! Come with me."

She led them into her **matchmaking** office, where Ember and Wade sat across from Cinder. On the table between them lay two sticks.

"I will splash this on your heart to bring love to the **surface**," Cinder explained. She splashed Ember with oil, a little **forcefully**.

Then Cinder splashed Wade, leaving an oil slick[4] on his watery surface. Wade **flinch**ed, but then felt a **pleasant sensation**.

Cinder gestured toward the sticks. "And then you must light these with your fire and I will read the smoke."

Ember lit one stick with her **flaming** finger. But Wade **gulp**ed and looked at his finger. He had no way to light the flame.

"See, Ember?" said Cinder. "It cannot be."

"Actually . . . ," said Wade **thoughtfully**. He moved until he stood between Ember and the sticks.

"What are you doing?" Ember **whisper**ed.

Wade pulled up his shirt. His clear, watery surface

---

4   oil slick 유막. 기름으로 된 얇은 막.

refracted Ember's light, as if he were a **magnifying glass**. When he focused the **beam** of light onto the stick, the stick **burst** into flames.

Both Cinder and Ember **blink**ed with surprise.

The **intermingling** smoke from the sticks turned into a double helix.[5] Cinder sniffed the smoke as it rose. Ember watched it, too. Could the smoke actually tell them something?

"Cinder?" Bernie called from upstairs. "Cinder? Who's down there?"

Ember was **horrified**. "It's my dad. You have to go!" She and Cinder **rush**ed Wade out the door just as Bernie came downstairs.

"Wait, are we a **match**?" Wade asked as the door closed. When his hand got caught, he **yelp**ed and pulled it out. Then he **reluctantly** headed home.

"What's going on?" asked Bernie. "I woke up and nobody was upstairs!"

"It was just me," said Ember. "I was . . . double-checking the locks. And Mom came down, and . . ."

---

5   **double helix** 이중 나선. 서로 대칭인 두 가닥의 얇은 선이 서로 뒤틀리면서 얽혀 있는 모양.

"Yes, and we . . . ," Cinder said, her eyes **dart**ing around the room, "began looking at this door. We don't talk about this door enough!"

"Pull it together!" Ember hissed at her mother.

Bernie smiled. "Well, since you are awake . . . I was going to tell you tomorrow, but I'm too excited to sleep. In two days, I retire!"

"Oh!" said Ember.

Cinder gasped. "Oh, Bernie!"

"Two days?" asked Ember with a gulp.

"Yes," said Bernie. "We are going to throw a *big* party. A grand **reopening**! That way I can tell the whole world my daughter is taking over."

Cinder **clap**ped, **overjoyed**, but Ember could only smile weakly.

Bernie took Cinder by the hand and spun her around.

"And I have a gift for you," Bernie announced to Ember. "I've had this for a while, but after our talk, I know now is the time." He pulled out a large box from behind the **counter**. Then his face grew serious. "Before I give it to you, I need you to understand what it means to me."

Bernie **recall**ed the day when he and Cinder had **board**ed a boat that would take them to Element City. "When I left Fire Land," he began, "I gave my father the *'Bà Ksô,'* the Big Bow. It is the highest form of **respect**. But my father did not return the Bow, he did not give me his **blessing**. He said if we left Fire Land, we would lose who we are."

"They never got to see all of this," Bernie sadly continued, gesturing around his shop. "They didn't get to see that I *never* forgot we are Fire. This is a **burden** I still carry."

Cinder's eyes **well**ed up with tears.

"Ember," said Bernie, "it is important that you know you have *my* blessing every day you come in here. So I had this made for you."

He opened the **package** and **reveal**ed a sign that read EMBER'S FIREPLACE.

Ember was **stunned**. "Wow, *Àshfá,*" she said, her eyes wide.

Bernie **flare**d up, full of **youthful** energy. "It's gonna be big, bright! Everyone is gonna see this. Ember's Fireplace! We will **unveil** it at the grand reopening!" He **chuckle**d happily.

Cinder, fearing Bernie might **exhaust** himself, took him

by the hand. "Come, Bernie, you need your rest," she said. She **shot** Ember a look as they passed.

Ember sat on the floor, alone in the shop, staring at the sign. Her flame **dim**med as she began to quietly cry.

Across town, a wave of water spilled into the culvert. The glass dam Ember had created still held, but the water had risen nearly to the top. Under the **pressure** of the **immense** amount of water, a **tiny** crack appeared in the tempered glass.

Chapter 15

The next day, Wade heard a knock on the door of his mother's apartment. He opened it and was **thrilled** to see Ember, who was holding a box.

"Ember!" he said. "So, what'd your mom say? About our reading?"

"Nothing," she said. "Look, I have a gift for you." She waved him into the hall, and then she handed him the box.

Wade reached in and **gently** pulled out the Vivisteria glass. He **stared** at it, still **mesmerized** by its beauty. "And you came all the way here to give it to me?" he **murmured**. Then he noticed the sad **expression** on her face. "Wait, why are you giving me gifts?"

When Ember looked away, Wade suddenly sensed she was here to end things. "Oh, no," he said sadly. His eyes fell to the Vivisteria glass, and then he remembered something.

"Hold on," Wade said quickly. "I think I have something to show you. Just give me two seconds! I have to call Gale! And you're going to need a pair of **boot**s!"

Soon after, Wade led Ember toward the **deserted** Garden Central Station. Along the way, they passed a **faded** sign **advertising** the Vivisteria flower—the same sign Ember had seen when she was little. Now the sign had a **banner** across it, announcing that the **exhibit** was closed.

"Wade, what are we doing here?" asked Ember.

"Just wait!" said Wade. He stopped in front of a chain-link fence.[1] When he took off his shirt, he was able to walk right through the fence.

Ember walked through the fence, too, but when she did it, she **melt**ed the metal.

"Why do they even have these?" asked Wade.

---

1   chain-link fence 철책. 굵은 철사를 다이아몬드 모양으로 엮어서 만든 울타리.

"Eh, who knows," said Ember.

They hurried toward the station. A sign that read NO FIRE still stood in the **entryway**, keeping Fire Elements out. Wade **knock**ed it over as he passed.

The train station had clearly been closed for a very long time. Only a few **ornate** tiles remained on the walls. Water **drip**ped from the **ceiling**, and the entrance stairs **vanish**ed into a dark, **flooded** tunnel.

There, in front of the tunnel, stood Gale. She waved. "Hey! It's my favorite fireball!"

Puzzled, Ember waved back. "Hey, Gale." She glanced at Wade. "What's going on?"

"I know you think you have to end this," he began, "but that flooded tunnel? It goes to the main terminal."

"Okay?" said Ember.

"Do you still want to see a Vivisteria?" Wade asked.

He gave Gale a **signal**. She **inhale**d deeply and blew a huge bubble in the water, big enough for Ember to climb into. Gale held the bubble closed at the water's **surface**.

Ember was **stunned**. "Wait, I'm supposed to get in there?" she asked.

"The air should last . . . ," said Wade.

". . . at least twenty minutes," Gale added.

Ember hesitated.

"*They* said you couldn't go in there . . . ," said Wade. "Why does *anyone* get to tell you what you can do in your life?"

Ember's **brow furrow**ed. She looked at the bubble. Then she looked at Wade. She stepped to the **edge** of the water.

Gale blew even more air into the bubble, and Ember jumped in. Gale **seal**ed it so no water could **leak** inside. Then Ember **steadied** herself and looked out at Wade, who gave her two thumbs up. It was working!

Wade gently **grab**bed the bubble and started swimming down the flooded staircase. From the surface, Gale waved goodbye.

With Ember in her **protective** bubble, Wade swam through the dark tunnel. Surrounded by water, Ember started to panic a little. But she remembered that Wade was by her side and she felt calmer.

On the other side of the tunnel was the old train station. Inside the station, Ember's light **illuminate**d the walls. This part of the station was **gorgeous**. Somehow **preserve**d underwater, the tiles were still beautiful, and so was the **vaulted** ceiling overhead, **crisscross**ed with green trellises.[2]

When Wade and Ember **explore**d an old subway car, her glow **startle**d a **school** of fish. As the fish **swirl**ed around her bubble, she laughed.

They followed the fish up a staircase, which opened into a **grand ballroom**. In the middle, growing in a double helix, rested the Vivisteria plant.

The **dormant** plant was without any flowers. But as Wade pushed Ember closer and her light illuminated the **vine**, it **bloom**ed!

"A Vivisteria," whispered Ember. It was even more beautiful than she had imagined. As she floated up the vine, her light cast colorful prisms,[3] and more flowers bloomed.

Ember gazed at the **purplish** red blossoms—until another school of fish sent her bubble spinning. "Whoa!" she cried, laughing.

As she laughed, her flames grew brighter, and even more

---

2 **trellis** 격자(格子). 바둑판처럼 가로세로를 일정한 간격으로 직각이 되게 만든 구조물.

3 **prism** 프리즘. 빛을 분산시키거나 굴절시키기 위해 만들어진 삼각기둥 모양의 장치. 여기에서는 빛을 프리즘에 통과시켜 분산시키면 나타나는 무지개 색을 가리키는 말로 쓰였다.

flowers bloomed! Ember **lit up** with joy, and the vine **exploded** with flowers. She and Wade continued to swim through the beautiful vines, sharing the magical moment.

But suddenly, the bubble around Ember began to **shrink**.

The flames on the top of her head were now touching the inside of the bubble. "Ouch!" she cried.

"Hey!" Wade gasped. "You're **run**ning **out** of air!" He **frantically** searched for an exit. "That way," he declared. He pushed Ember's bubble toward a narrow **stairwell**.

As the bubble **tighten**ed, Ember started to **pant**, taking short little gasps of air.

"Almost there," said Wade. "Try to breathe slow and steady." He pushed her bubble upward, swimming with all his **strength**.

Finally, they saw light. They broke through the old subway entrance just **in time, land**ing on the **sidewalk** near Mineral Lake and **collapsing**.

As they lay **side by side**, Wade's eyes were wide with **regret**. "I'm so sorry," he said. "I should never have—"

Ember **sprang** to her feet. "Are you kidding?" she said. "That was *amazing*. I finally saw a Vivisteria!"

"It was **inspiring**," Wade agreed. "*You* were inspiring." He held out his hand, his gaze steady.

Ember turned away. "No, Wade, we can't touch," she said.

"Maybe we *can*," he said.

Ember stared at the lake. "No," she said again.

"But can't we just **prove** it?" Wade **plead**ed.

She glanced at him. "Prove what?"

"Let's see what happens," he said, throwing his arms wide, "and if it's a **disaster**, then we'll know this would never work."

"But it actually *could* be a disaster," Ember **remind**ed him, her voice rising. "I could **vaporize** you. You could **extinguish** me. And then—"

Wade **cut** her **off**. "Let's . . . let's start small." He held out his hand again.

Ember hesitated. Then she **tentatively** reached toward it, **hover**ing her hand over his. When Wade's hand began to bubble, Ember **yank**ed hers back.

But they tried again. This time, they were able to touch— pressing their **palm**s together. Water boiled and **steam hiss**ed. But they were okay.

Ember gasped. She pulled her hand away and **examine**d

it. Wade studied his hand, too. They were **amazed**.

They stepped closer and pressed their palms together again, more **firmly** this time. Wade's water pushed back to match the strength of Ember's heat. Their hands **tingle**d as they **interlock**ed fingers. They had reached an **equilibrium**. *They had changed each other's* **chemistry***!*

In that magical moment, in each other's arms, they began to dance.

Wade **lean**ed into Ember and closed his eyes. "I'm so lucky," he whispered.

Those words **spark**ed a memory in Ember. Someone else had said similar words to her—her father. "I'm so lucky I have you," Bernie had said that night in the shop.

She could **picture** him standing beside the Blue Flame with her, a proud smile on his face. Then she remembered how **exhausted** he was. He couldn't go on like this for much longer.

The sign Bernie had given Ember **flash**ed on and off in her mind: EMBER'S FIREPLACE.

At that thought, Ember zipped up her fire, covering her beautiful, **vulnerable** light. She pulled away from Wade. "I have to go," she said.

"Wait, what?" asked Wade with **confusion**. "Where are you going?" When she hurried up the Wetro stairs, he followed.

"Back to my life at the shop," Ember said. "Where I belong. I **take over** tomorrow."

Wade jumped in front of her. "Whoa, whoa, hold up. You don't *want* that. You said so yourself!"

"It doesn't matter what I want," Ember replied weakly.

"Of course it does!" cried Wade.

She darted around him, up the Wetro stairs, but Wade followed. "Listen," he called after her. "*Listen!* You've got an **opportunity** to do something you *want* with your life!"

She **whirl**ed around on the station **platform**. *"Want?"* she **repeat**ed. "Yeah, that may work in your rich-kid, follow-your-heart family. But getting to 'do what you want' is a **luxury**. And not for people like me."

"Why not?" asked Wade. "Just tell your father how you feel. This is too important. Maybe he'll agree."

Ember rolled her eyes. "Oh, ha. Yeah." There was **absolutely** no way she would do that.

Wade **set his jaw**. "Funny," he said. "And this whole time I thought you were so strong, but it turns out . . . you're just afraid."

His words **ignite**d Ember's fire. "**Don't you** *dare* judge me," she said. "You don't know what it's like to have parents who **gave up** *everything* for you."

Wade looked at her sadly.

"I'm *Fire,* Wade," Ember continued. "I can't be anything more than that. It's what I am, and what my *family* is. It's our way of *life*. I cannot throw all of that away just for *you*."

All Wade could say was "I don't understand."

Ember **glower**ed. "And that alone is a reason this could never work. It's over, Wade." A train pulled into the station and she quickly boarded it, leaving Wade alone on the platform.

But inside the train, she stopped short. She took a **shaky** breath, trying to **hold back** her tears. Then she armored up, pulling her hood tightly over her flames.

Chapter 16

The night of the shop's **grand reopening** party, a stage stood outside the shop, lit by hanging lights. The whole **community gather**ed for the big event. Customers sat at **outdoor** tables, **snack**ing on hot kol nuts.

Bernie wanted everything to be perfect. He had even closed the shop for a few days to prepare.

Ember, in a **ceremonial** gown,[1] sat on the stage with Cinder. Bernie carried the Blue **Flame** lantern and placed it on a **pedestal nearby**.

---

1 **gown** 가운. 특별한 의식이나 행사 때에 입는 헐렁하고 긴 겉옷.

"Everyone, welcome!" Bernie said. "It is good to see your faces. I am **honored** to have **serve**d you. But it is time to move on." He gestured toward Ember. "Come."

Ember stood next to her father.

"My daughter, you are the Ember of our family fire," Bernie said **affectionately**. "That is why I am so proud to have you **take over** my life's work."

He touched a rope, which burned like a fuse[2] toward a tarp covering the new sign on the front of the shop. For a moment, it looked as if the entire shop was **ablaze**. But when the smoke **clear**ed, Ember's sign glowed in all its **glory**.

As the **audience cheer**ed, Bernie looked at Ember. "Pretty good **trick**, huh?" he said. Then he held out the Blue Flame lantern. "This is the lantern I brought from our old country. Today I pass it on to you."

As Ember reached for the lantern, she **hesitate**d, feeling the **weight** of the moment. But just as she was about to take it, she heard a familiar voice.

"I thought of other reasons," someone called.

---

2 **fuse** 도화선. 폭죽이나 폭약 등을 터지게 하기 위해서 불을 붙이는 심지.

Ember looked up to see a train passing. Then she noticed Wade standing in front of her and gasped.

"Wade?" she said, shocked.

The members of the crowd murmured to one another.

Cinder **swallow**ed hard. "Oh, boy," she said under her breath.

"What are you doing here?" Ember asked.

"You said me not understanding is the reason we can never work," explained Wade, choosing his words carefully. "But I thought of other reasons. A **bunch** of them. Like, number one: you're Fire, I'm Water. I mean, come on. That's crazy, right?"

A Fire **Element** in the audience **nod**ded in **agreement**.

"Who is this?" Bernie asked.

"No idea," Cinder **fib**bed **unconvincingly**.

"Number two," Wade said, "I'm **crash**ing your party. Like, what kind of a jerk³ am I?"

"A pretty big one," **admit**ted Ember.

"Right?" said Wade. "Number three: I can't eat your . . . delicious foods!" To **demonstrate**, he took a **mug** from one

---

3 jerk '바보', '얼간이'라는 뜻의 속어.

of the outdoor tables. He swallowed its **contents** and **strain**ed to speak, his head bubbling with the heat. *"Very* **unpleasant**," he **croak**ed.

Bernie suddenly **recognize**d Wade. "Wait, I know him!" he said to Cinder. "He is the food **inspector**!"

"Oh, right!" Wade continued. "Number four: I'm **ban**ned from your father's shop. There are a *million* reasons why this can't work. A million no's. But there's also one 'yes.' "

He stepped closer to Ember. "We touched," he said. "And when we did, something happened to us. Something *impossible*. We changed each other's **chemistry**."

As he **gaze**d into Ember's eyes, she smiled.

But Bernie jumped toward them, **exasperated**. "Enough!" he cried, his voice yanking Ember back to reality. "What kind of food **inspection** is this?"

Wade **stood his ground**. "A food inspection of the heart, sir," he replied.

"Who are you?" asked Bernie, **jab**bing his **fiery** finger at Wade.

"Just a guy who burst into your daughter's life in a **flooded** old **basement**," Wade said.

"So you *are* the one who burst the pipes!" **accuse**d Bernie.

"What?" said Wade, taken aback. "Not me, it was . . ." His eyes **involuntarily dart**ed toward Ember.

Ember's eyes **widen**ed. It was too late. The **damage** had been done.

Bernie looked sadly at Ember. "You?" he asked, his eyes **narrow**ing. "*You* burst the pipe?"

"I—I—" **stammer**ed Ember.

"Ember—" Wade started to say.

"Silence!" Bernie **bellow**ed.

"No!" cried Wade. He pleaded with Ember. "Take the chance. Let your father know who you really are."

Ember was **speechless**.

"Look," said Wade. "I had regrets when my dad died, but because of you, I've learned to **embrace** the light while it burns." Then he **recite**d in perfect Firish: "*Tìshók'*. You don't have forever to say what you need to say. I love you, Ember Lumen."

Party guests gasped, but Wade continued. "And I'm pretty sure you love me, too," he said softly.

Ember looked into Wade's eyes. She **was** completely **torn**, but she had to make a decision. She put up her fire wall, trying to hide behind it.

"No, Wade," she said **flatly**. "I don't."

At that moment, in the **culvert**, the crack in Ember's glass dam grew larger.

Wade's heart felt as if it were cracking, too.

"That's not true!" Cinder argued with Ember. Then she faced Bernie. "I did their reading!" Cinder **confess**ed, throwing her arms in the air. "Bernie, it's love. It's true love."

"No, Mom," said Ember, "you're wrong. Wade, go!"

"But, Ember—" he **protest**ed.

Ember flared as hotly as she ever had. "I don't love you!" she **holler**ed.

At this, another crack **slice**d through the glass wall. Water started to **spray** out. Any moment now, the dam would blow.

"Go!" Ember cried again, purple with anger.

Wade, **heartbroken**, removed the glass Vivisteria from his pocket. He placed it on the stage at Ember's feet. Then he walked away, his shoulders **sag**ging.

Bernie **glare**d at Ember. "You have been seeing *Water*?"

"*Àshfá,* I—" she tried.

Hurt and **betrayal flicker**ed across Bernie's face. "You caused the leak in the shop?" he said. "I *trusted* you!"

Ember's flames burned with **shame**.

Bernie began to **cough**. "You will not take over the shop. I no longer **retire**." He grabbed the lantern and **storm**ed into the shop, with Cinder following close behind.

Ember stood alone onstage as party guests began to quietly leave, their **subdued** flames **disappear**ing into the **dusk**. She stared sadly at the glass Vivisteria.

When the guests were gone, Ember was **consume**d with sadness. She climbed onto her scooter. She drove through Firetown and onto the bridge. She parked, removed her ceremonial gown, and stared at the bright lights of Element City **in the distance**.

Ember remembered the moment when she and Wade had touched for the first time—how they had danced at Mineral Lake. She pulled the glass Vivisteria from her pocket and **sigh**ed. Then she looked back at Firetown. "Why can't I just be a good daughter?" she asked herself **aloud**.

Her **frustration** flared, and she wound back her arm to throw the Vivisteria into the water. But she couldn't bring herself to do it.

Ember stared again at her mirror image in the glass Vivisteria. She could see parts of Element City and Firetown in the glass, too. Suddenly, a **flash** of light **reflect**ed in the Vivisteria. It was coming from the culvert in the distance.

"Firetown!" Ember cried.

The glass wall she had built at the dam had **shatter**ed— she was certain of it.

Pent-up water began gushing down the culvert, straight toward Firetown. A **deluge** was **head**ed for her father's shop.

Ember raced to her scooter and **took off**.

Chapter 17

Inside Grand Gateway station, Wade purchased a ticket. "Well, **one-way** ticket to anywhere but here," he said sadly.

His family had **gather**ed to say goodbye. "Go! Travel the world. Heal that broken heart," **blubber**ed Brook. Then she began to sing. "My little drip-drip baby boy. Drip, drip, drip goes the baby boy. . . ."

Wade's eyes **well**ed up.

Harold started crying, too. "I made you a painting," he said. "It's of a lonely man **awash** in sadness."

The painting **depict**ed Wade, standing at the station, just as he was right now. Wade **burst** into tears.

Through a doorway, he **spot**ted steam rising from Firetown. One by one, the lights of the town **flicker**ed out. "Ember," Wade **murmur**ed. Was she in trouble?

Ember was already racing her scooter back across the bridge toward Firetown. Down below, she could see her parents in front of the shop, cleaning up from the party. "Mom! Dad!" she cried. But they couldn't hear her.

A wall of water **rush**ed down the **culvert**. The river **slam**med into the **elevated** Wetro track, which came **crash**ing down.

Ember **pull**ed **off** from the bridge and **race**d the **raging** river toward the shop. But now water was filling the street!

She **rev**ved the scooter and bravely **soar**ed across the culvert. "Water's coming!" she **holler**ed to any Fire Elements in her path. "**Watch out!** Behind you!"

All around her, Fire Elements began to **panic** and run to **safety**.

"Climb! Climb!" Ember cried, **urging** them toward higher

ground. "Flash flood!**¹** Hurry!"

As she **near**ed the shop, she shouted to her parents. "Mom! Water! Get to higher ground!"

Cinder, who was helping Bernie clean up the stage area from the **grand reopening, instantly grab**bed Bernie. She **tug**ged on him to go.

Then Ember's scooter **hydroplane**d, with waves **splash**ing upward. It sent a **streak** of pain up her leg. The water in the street was getting too deep to ride her scooter. She **leap**ed off it and onto the **cab** of a pickup truck. Would she be able to reach the shop from here?

Water lifted the stage, carrying Bernie and Cinder with it. Bernie **lunge**d toward the shop. "The Flame!" he cried.

Cinder held him back.

"Let me go!" **yell**ed Bernie.

Then he saw Ember jump onto **float**ing **debris** that carried her toward the shop. She was **risk**ing her life to save the Flame.

"Ember, no!" he cried.

---

1 **flash flood** 돌발 홍수. 지대가 낮거나 면적이 좁은 유역에 집중적인 강우가 발생하면서, 하천에 유입되는 물의 양이 짧은 기간에 급증하는 현상.

She took one more leap through an open window above the shop's front door. Water was already **gush**ing in.

Crack!

Ember **gasp**ed as the front door began to give way. **Spout**s of water **jet**ted in around the door, flowing toward the Blue Flame.

Ember threw her **weight** against the door. The rising water **nip**ped painfully at her feet.

Suddenly, through the glass of the door, two eyes appeared. Ember heard a **muffled grunt**. "Wade?" she said.

His face **materialize**d, **smush**ed against the glass. He **gesture**d toward the door handle. "**Keyhole**!" he cried in a muffled voice.

Ember yanked the key from the **lock**, and Wade **squeeze**d in through the keyhole. "Gahhh!" he cried.

Inside the shop, he **reform**ed his body. "I was hoping to make a more **heroic entrance**," he said.

Then he **sprang into action**, joining Ember at the door. **Side by side**, they **held back** the wall of water.

"You came back after everything I said," said Ember.

"Are you kidding? And miss all this?" he joked.

Ember smiled—until she saw that the rising water in the shop had nearly reached the Blue Flame. "Hold the door!" she cried.

Ember jumped along **counter**s and **shelves** until she reached the Flame. She **pile**d sandbags around the base of the **cauldron**. Then she **flare**d up and made glass from the **melt**ed sand.

Outside the shop, Bernie and Cinder **clung** to the stage as **violent** water **churn**ed all around them. Debris rushed down the street, **smash**ing cars and knocking down street lamps. The sign **tumble**d off the front of Bernie's shop, narrowly missing them.

Back inside, as water rose, Ember quickly built a glass **cylinder** around the Blue Flame. "No, no," she **plead**ed, hoping the glass would hold.

Wade **struggle**d to hold the door **in place** as windows and pipes began to burst. Water rose faster, covering the family photos on the wall. The lantern that had carried the Blue Flame from Fire Land was **swept** up in the flow.

"Ember, we have to go!" cried Wade. "We have to go *now!*"

"I can't leave!" cried Ember.

"I'm sorry to say this," said Wade, "but the shop is done. The Flame is done."

"No!" cried Ember. "This is my father's whole life. I'm not going anywhere—"

Smash! Water **roar**ed through a **brick** wall. A shelf **topple**d and slammed into the glass cylinder, breaking the glass and **exposing** the Flame.

The base was cracked, the Flame weak. But it wasn't out. Ember climbed up on a box to avoid the rising water. "Throw me that lantern!" she shouted.

Wade spun in a circle, searching, and then swam for the lantern. Then a huge wave swept him sideways. "Ah!"

The wave pushed Ember and the base of the Blue Flame toward the old fireplace **hearth**. Debris piled up, **seal**ing Ember inside. She **grip**ped the base of the Flame, but when she **glance**d down, she saw that the Flame was **extinguish**ed.

"No!" cried Ember.

Just then, the debris shifted. Wade **pop**ped into the hearth, and he was holding something. It was the lantern—with the Blue Flame inside! Wade handed it to Ember.

"Thank you," breathed Ember. "Thank you." Then she

flinched in pain. "Ahhh!"

Water had **seep**ed into the hearth and splashed onto Ember's knees. She studied the blocked entrance and saw water **trickling** in through the cracks.

Ember used her heat to melt the debris and seal the cracks. Her efforts stopped the **leak**s, but also created a lot of heat. It was now so warm in the hearth, Wade began to boil.

"It's too hot in here," he said.

Ember looked up at the **chimney stack**, which opened to the sky above. "Climb!" she ordered. She went first, and Wade followed.

But before they could reach the top, a car **cascade**d down the water-filled street and crashed into the shop, shaking the building. The top of the chimney **collapse**d, sealing Wade and Ember inside.

The space was so small, so tight, and so very hot. "Back up! Back up! *Back up!*" cried Ember.

They dropped back down into the hearth, which was even tighter, now that more debris had fallen. Wade was steaming.

Ember went over to the blocked entrance. She heated up again, trying to burn through. It didn't work. And now the room was even hotter.

Wade was **evaporating** at an **alarming rate**.

"I have to open that up!" cried Ember.

"No!" said Wade. "The water will come in, and you'll be **snuff**ed out."

"But you're evaporating!" cried Ember. She saw that Wade was **full-on** boiling now. "I don't know what to do!"

"It's okay," he said calmly.

"No, it's not okay!" she cried.

He took her hand. "Ember, I have no **regret**s," he said. "You gave me something people search for their whole lives."

Ember cried, pleading with him. "But I can't exist in a world without you! I'm sorry I didn't say it before. I love you, Wade."

Steam **surround**ed them.

In her **sorrow**, Ember's most **vulnerable** light **cast** rainbows on the wall.

Wade instantly felt a sense of peace. "I really do love it when your light does that," he **whisper**ed.

As they **embrace**d, steam continued to fill the hearth.

Silence fell.

Wade was gone.

Chapter 18

When the water **receded**, Bernie, Cinder, and their neighbors pushed through the **damp debris, desperate** to find Ember.

"They're in the **hearth!**" cried a Fire **Element**.

They cleared debris away from the fireplace, **knock**ed through an **opening**, and found Ember.

She **knelt** on broken **brick**s and glass, **illuminate**d by the **flicker** of the Blue **Flame**. Her own light was **dim**. "Wade is gone," she said sadly.

Cinder climbed in and held Ember tight. "Oh, my daughter," she **soothe**d.

"He saved me," said Ember. She pulled out of Cinder's

embrace and faced her father.

"Dad . . . this is my fault," Ember said, her voice **shaky**. "The shop, Wade . . . I need to tell you the truth."

She **took a** deep **breath**. It was time to **admit** what she had come to **realize**. "I don't want to run the shop. I know that was your dream, but it's not mine. I'm sorry. I'm a bad daughter."

She handed the lantern with the Blue Flame to her father.

Bernie set down the lantern. "Ember, the shop was never the dream," he said, his voice **thick**. "*You* were the dream. You were always the dream."

At those words, Ember embraced her father. "I loved him, Dad," she admitted, **sob**bing now.

Cinder wrapped her arms around them, too. Then Ember heard a familiar **whimper**.

Condensation[1] had formed in the **chimney**.

A drop of water, like a single tear, fell into a **bucket**. Ember **glance**d up. Could it be?

Then Ember got an idea. She remembered the Crying

---

1   **condensation** 응결. 기체가 액체로 변하는 것으로, 공기가 냉각되면서 수증기가 물방울로 맺히는 현상.

Game she had played with Wade and his family. "Butterfly . . . ," she said softly. She **stare**d hopefully at the chimney. "Butterfly. **Windshield** wipers. Half a butterfly."

She could hear Wade crying softly now. A few more drops **plunk**ed into the bucket.

Ember felt a **surge** of hope. "An old man on his **deathbed** remembers the summer he fell in love . . . ," she said brightly.

More drops fell.

Ember covered her mouth, crying tears of joy this time. "She was out of his **league**, and he was young and **scared**," she continued. "He let her go thinking surely summer would come again. It never did."

Water fell harder now. Wade was **bawl**ing.

Realization dawned in Cinder's eyes as she **gaze**d upward. "You are a perfect **match**," she **announce**d. "Ten out of ten!"

Wade sobbed. As water **pour**ed into the bucket, Bernie looked at Cinder. "I don't understand," he said. "What's going on?"

Cinder waved her hand. "Just say something to make the Water guy cry, okay?"

Bernie **scratch**ed his head. "Um, uh . . . you are no longer panned," he said.

"**Ban**ned," Wade whimpered.

"Banned," Bernie agreed.

As Wade **wail**ed, a **puddle** formed on the ground. Ember stepped over to the middle of it. "I want to **explore** the world with you, Wade Ripple!" she shouted. "I want to have you with me, in my life. Forever!"

Droplets poured down, and then they stopped. The bucket was full. Ember **peer**ed into the bucket.

Two eyes peered back. And a smile formed.

Wade stood up. "Whoa," he breathed, suddenly realizing he wasn't wearing any clothes. "Your, uh, chimney needs cleaning." He quickly **locate**d his shirt and pulled it on.

Ember ran toward Wade, laughing. They kissed for the very first time. Ember **glow**ed a **breathtaking** purple that **lit up** the room.

"I *knew* it!" **declare**d Cinder, **beam**ing. "My nose *always* knows."

Even Bernie had to **chuckle**. Ember looked so happy. How could he not be happy for her?

It took many months for Firetown to **recover** from the flood. Bernie's shop, now fully **restore**d, **bustle**d with customers. The original shop sign hung above the door. Hot **log**s spun, **lava** java **steam**ed, and kids **crunch**ed on **crackly** candy.

Clod, wearing a shop **apron**, stood on a **ladder** beside a Fire girl. "If you were a vegetable," he said, "you'd be a cute-cumber.[2]" He held up his arm and **reveal**ed an **armpit** flower. He **yank**ed it out, **yelp**ing in pain, and presented it to the girl. "My queen."

She **giggle**d.

Gale, dressed in a Windbreakers jersey, **browse**d the **merchandise**. "Uh! I can't believe I was gonna **shut** this place **down**," she said.

As she gazed at the **stock**ed **shelves**, she **accidentally** backed up into an **Earth** guy who was also wearing a Windbreakers jersey.

"Whoa! Sorry," Gale **apologize**d. Then she realized who

---

2 cute-cumber 'cucumber(오이)'의 앞부분에 발음이 비슷한 'cute(귀여운)'를 넣은 말장난.

it was. "Fern? You're a Windbreakers fan?"

"Toot, toot," he answered, **pump**ing his **fist**.

"Toot, tooooot," said Gale, **instantly smitten**.

Flarry and Flarrietta stood behind the **counter** now. "Oy, you know what I like best about running this shop?" asked Flarrietta.

"Not having to eat Bernie's kol nuts!" declared Flarry, chuckling.

"Sorry, I couldn't hear you through my **retirement**," toyed Bernie.

Everyone **burst** out laughing just as Ember entered the shop. When Bernie caught her eye, they shared a smile.

Wade came in behind her. "Hey!"

Everyone **greet**ed him, **including** Bernie. "Hi, Wade!" they called **good-naturedly**.

"Hey, Wade!" called Clod. "Yo, yo, yo!"

Wade laughed and turned to Ember. "Ember, it's time," he said.

She smiled sadly, but she knew he was right. It was time to go.

At the **dock**s of the **Grand** Gateway, Ember and Wade prepared to **board** a **passenger** ship. But first they had to say goodbye to their families.

"You know, I'm not really one for tearful goodbyes," said Wade.

Brook burst out crying. "Oh, Wade," she **blubber**ed, "you big liar. **Drip**, drip, drip goes the baby boy." She hugged him.

As Wade burst into tears, too, Bernie **shot** Ember a glance. "Uh, are you sure about this one?" he asked.

Ember **grin**ned. "I'm sure." Then her **expression** changed. "Dad, I'm sorry the internship is so far away. I mean, it's the best glass-design company in the world, but who knows if it'll become a real job. And it might not **end up** being anything—"

"Shh," said Bernie. "Go. Start a new life. Your mother and I will be here. And now we have more time for hanky-panky."

"*Ê . . . shútsh!*" **scold**ed Cinder, giving him a playful **nudge**.

Wade and Ember began to walk up the ramp[3] of the ship,

---

3 ramp 램프. 승객과 화물이 쉽게 이동할 수 있도록 육지와 선박을 연결하는 완만한 경사로.

but Ember turned back. She smiled at Bernie and set down her **luggage**. Then she knelt on the dock. She **stretch**ed her arms out long before her and gave Bernie the *Bà Ksô,* the Big **Bow**.

Cinder **gasp**ed at the **respectful gesture**. But Bernie, tears in his eyes, stepped forward and returned the bow. He and Ember shared a moment, both feeling a **tremendous weight** lift. Then Cinder helped Bernie up, and the boat sounded its **horn**.

It was time for Ember and Wade to go.

Ember hurried up the ramp and boarded the boat behind Wade. Leaving Firetown was difficult, but she had taken the first step long ago—when she had **summon**ed up the **courage** to follow a Water man onto a train.

Leaving her parents and the **security** of their family shop was even more difficult. What was ahead for her, across these waters? What did the future hold? Ember didn't know. But with Wade by her side, she was ready to find out.